The Study and
Teaching of Sociology

James A. Kitchens

North Texas State University

Raymond H. Muessig

The Ohio State University

Charles E. Merrill Publishing Company
A Bell & Howell Company
Columbus   Toronto   London   Sydney

The Study and Teaching of Social Science Series
Raymond H. Muessig, Editor

Published by Charles E. Merrill Publishing Co.
A Bell & Howell Company
Columbus, Ohio 43216

This book was set in Souvenir
Cover Design Coordination: Will Chenoweth
Production Coordination: Linda Hillis Bayma

Credits: Specific acknowledgments of permissions to use materials appear on page iv, which is to be considered an extension of this copyright page. Standard credit and source information appears in the *Notes.*

Photos: Cover by Gene Gilliom; Rohn Engh, 12, 17 (middle left), 35, 49 (right), 51; Larry Hammill, 17 (middle right), 25, 49 (left); Ronald W. Henderson, 17 (top); *Values in the Classroom* (Charles E. Merrill, 1977), 17 (bottom).

Library of Congress Catalog Card Number: 79-89620

International Standard Book Number: 0–675–08194-7

1 2 3 4 5 6 7 8 9 10—85 84 83 82 81 80

Printed in the United States of America

To the Nubian, peaceful
and gentle — an example to me.

Acknowledgments

From GENDER AND SEX IN SOCIETY by Lucile Duberman. Copyright © 1975 by Praeger Publishers, Inc. Reprinted by permission of Holt, Rinehart and Winston.

Excerpts from THE BEST CHRISTMAS PAGEANT EVER by Barbara Robinson. Text copyright © 1972 by Barbara Robinson. Courtesy of Harper & Row, Publishers, Inc.

From PISTOL by Adrienne Richard, by permission of Little, Brown and Co. in association with the Atlantic Monthly Press. Copyright © 1965, 1969 by Adrienne Richard.

A selection from NOBODY'S FAMILY IS GOING TO CHANGE by Louise Fitzhugh. Copyright © 1974 by Louise Fitzhugh. Reprinted with the permission of Farrar, Straus & Giroux, Inc.

From CARLOTA by Scott O'Dell. Copyright © 1977 by Houghton Mifflin Co. Reprinted by permission of Houghton Mifflin Co.

From NO MORE SCHOOL by Howard S. Rowland. Copyright © 1975 by Howard S. Rowland. Reprinted by permission of the publisher, Elsevier-Dutton.

Reprinted by permission of G. P. Putnam's Sons from MY LIFE by Golda Meir. Copyright © 1975 by Golda Meir.

From NIGGER: AN AUTOBIOGRAPHY by Dick Gregory, with Robert Lipsyte. Copyright © 1964 by Dick Gregory Enterprises, Inc. Reprinted by permission of the publisher, E. P. Dutton.

Excerpt from PROBING THE UNKNOWN: The Story of Dr. Florence Sabin, written by Mary Kay Phelan. Copyright © 1969 by Mary Kay Phelan. By permission of Thomas Y. Crowell, Publishers.

Excerpts from "America's New Manners." Reprinted by permission from TIME, The Weekly Newsmagazine; Copyright Time Inc. 1978.

Excerpted from THE AMY VANDERBILT COMPLETE BOOK OF ETIQUETTE: A GUIDE TO CONTEMPORARY LIVING, By Amy Vanderbilt.* Copyright © 1978 by Curtis B. Kellar and Lincoln G. Clark, Executors of the Estate of Amy Vanderbilt Kellar and Doubleday & Company, Inc. Copyright © 1952, 1954, 1955, 1956, 1958, 1963, 1967, 1972 by Curtis B. Kellar and Lincoln G. Clark, Executors of the Estate of Amy Vanderbilt Kellar. Reprinted by permission of Doubleday & Company, Inc. *Revised and expanded by Letitia Baldridge.

From FEMALE & MALE: SOCIALIZATION, SOCIAL ROLES, AND SOCIAL STRUCTURE, 2d ed., by Clarice Stasz Stoll. Copyright © 1978 by Wm. C. Brown Co. Publishers. Reprinted by permission of Wm. C. Brown Co. Publishers.

From PASSAGES: PREDICTABLE CRISES OF ADULT LIFE by Gail Sheehy. Copyright © 1974, 1976 by Gail Sheehy. By permission of the publishers. All rights reserved.

From SUNDAY FATHER by John Neufeld. Copyright © 1976 by John Neufeld. Reprinted by arrangement with The New American Library, Inc.

Foreword

The Study and Teaching of Social Science Series is composed of six books, *The Study and Teaching of Anthropology*, *The Study and Teaching of Economics*, *The Study and Teaching of Geography*, *The Study and Teaching of History*, *The Study and Teaching of Political Science*, and *The Study and Teaching of Sociology*. In the larger part of every one of the six volumes, the social scientist was asked to deal with the nature and development of his field, goals of and purposes served by the discipline, tools and procedures employed by scholars, significant and helpful literature in the field, and fundamental questions asked and ideas generated by the academic area. Writers were challenged not only to provide solid subject matter but also to treat content in a clear, concise, interesting, useful manner.

Each of the six works in the series concludes with a chapter entitled "Suggested Methods for Teachers," which was written after reading and considering the complete manuscript by the individual social scientist.

In a number of ways, *The Study and Teaching of Social Science Series* resembles *The Social Science Seminar Series* (published in 1965) from which it is descended. The idea for *The Social Science Seminar Series* came to me in 1963, when the structure-of-the-disciplines approach in social studies education was receiving considerable attention in publications, meetings, and projects. At that time, social studies educators and supervisors and others were searching for substantive material concerned with the essence of academic disciplines and for down-to-earth ideas for specific classroom learning activities. They sought materials which would spell out and facilitate ways of translating abstract social science concepts and generalizations into concrete inquiry strategies that would be meaningful and appealing to children and youth. In the early sixties, some historians, economists, sociologists, anthropologists, political scientists, and geographers were trying to think of ways that others could teach respectable social science to elementary and secondary students about whom the academicians had little knowledge and with whom university scholars had no experience. And certain classroom teachers and others in professional education were informed with respect to human growth and development, child and adolescent psychology, theories of instruction in general and of social studies education in particular, day-to-day classroom organization and management, etcetera, and could work and relate well with younger pupils. These practitioners, however, readily admitted their lack of the kind of breadth and depth in all of the various social sciences necessary to do even an adequate job of defining and interpreting the disciplines. They frequently added that they had insufficient financial resources, time, energy, background in methods and media, creativity, and writing talent to produce for themselves and others the pages of requisite, appropriate, fresh, variegated, pedagogical alternatives needed to reach heterogeneous collections of learners at all instructional levels.

Thus, it seemed to me that a very real need could be met by a series of solid, practical, readable books where the content on each discipline would be written by a specialist in that social science and where the material on teaching strategies would be developed by a specialist in social studies education.

Now, some brief comments are appropriate regarding the revised and many completely new approaches for the last chapters in *The Study and Teaching of Social Science Series*.

The 1965 *Social Science Seminar Series* was designed primarily to assist K–12 teachers in the application of a structure-of-the-disciplines social studies theory in their classrooms. Since the needs and pursuits of the many users of the series have changed and become more diverse than they were in 1965, and since I, too, have changed in the ensuing years, this 1980 rendering is considerably more eclectic than its progenitor. Rarely is there a one-to-one relationship between a specific teaching method and a particular, overall theory of social studies education. Additionally, a myriad of instructional media may be matched with different philosophies and techniques. And, a single theory of social studies education need not be followed by an entire school district, by a whole school, by all of the teachers at the same grade level, or even by a given teacher throughout a school year with each of the students. The suggested methods in the last chapters of *The Study and Teaching of Social Science Series*, then, can be used as presented, modified to suit various classroom situations, adapted to complement different social studies theories, and altered to fit numerous goals and objectives. In the final analysis, a key test of a teaching method is the extent to which it touches the life of an individual learner in a meaningful way.

A Special Acknowledgment

When Charles E. Merrill Publishing Company expressed an interest in my plan to develop a series of texts in social science and invited me to submit a detailed proposal, I immediately asked Dr. Vincent R. Rogers (then at the University of Minnesota and now at the University of Connecticut) if he would join me as co-editor of the series and co-author of the chapters on instructional approaches. I worked with Professor Rogers on the refined plan that was sent to and approved by Merrill. Vin Rogers and I had written together previously in an easy, relaxed, compatible, mutually advantageous manner. We were both former classroom teachers who had become university professors of social studies education. We shared a feeling for the needs, interests, problems, and aspirations of students and teachers, had a serious commitment to the social sciences, and were familiar with a variety of instructional media. But, more than any other person I could find and attract as a co-worker on the endeavor, Rogers could translate significant ideas into functional, sequential, additive, meaningful, imaginative, enjoyable methods. Vin did his share throughout the entire undertaking, and he was responsible for the securing of all but one of the initial social science authors of the first version of this program. Our writing together on *The*

Social Science Seminar Series went swimmingly, and we emerged even better friends than before.

When Merrill requested that Dr. Rogers and I revise and create new material for our concluding chapters for the six books in *The Study and Teaching of Social Science Series*, I anticipated the pleasure of a collaboration again. However, Professor Rogers already had too many previous commitments to undertake something as time consuming and demanding as this effort, and he had to withdraw, unfortunately. True to his generous personal and professional nature, Professor Rogers told me to use any or all of the ideas he and I had developed separately and together about fifteen years ago. We blended so well in the sixties, and so many things have happened since that time, that I doubt whether I could easily distinguish between our original suggestions anyway. Thus, my sincere thanks to Vin for his contribution to the first series and to this second undertaking.

Raymond H. Muessig

Preface

I am a dedicated "people watcher." In crowded shopping center malls, at football games, at parties, walking across campus, even stalled in heavy traffic, I watch people. To me, human life is a fascinating and intriguing subject. I like to know what people are doing, even when they are not aware of doing it. And, I am curious about why they behave as they do. Sociology, it seems, is a hobby with me as well as my profession. And that is why I've enjoyed writing this book. It has been designed as an introductory statement on the nature and uses of sociology and has been written with the nonsociologist in mind. Because it is geared to people who will probably never be professional sociologists, it is an invitation to begin a new hobby.

The intent of this text is to present the discipline to individuals interested in sharpening their skills of people watching. A sincere attempt has been made to reduce technical jargon to a minimum and to write in as conversational a style as possible. The opening chapter presents a broad overview of the sociological perspective, discusses where the discipline came from, and tries to show how practicing sociologists go about their work. The next three chapters are concerned with some of the results of sociological inquiry into human behavior. Chapter 5 tries to answer the question, "Of what practical use is the study of sociology?"

It is spring as I write these words. The warm sun is popping the buds on my pecan tree and fuzzy little pods are pushing the pink blooms from my peach tree. I hear the birds chatter away, singing to each other and to whomever else wishes to listen. Today my life is calm. But not everyone is so fortunate as I. Life can be tumultuous and for some, even perhaps many, life is more sorrow than joy. Sociology helps reveal the conditions of life under which people live and the social fabric of which human life is made. Social forces far beyond the individual's control determine the daily events that individuals experience. As such, sociology can be a disturbing discipline to study. Human life conditions for many in this country and the majority of nations across the earth are tragic. It is, however, the nonsociologist who may take the data of sociology to help create a more humane world. That, above all, is my hope.

James A. Kitchens

Contents

one

The Science of Social Life

It was Aristotle who first said that humans are social animals. Human beings, it seems, are characterized by one indisputable common denominator—everywhere people live in groups. It is difficult to imagine a situation in which people live in isolation from all other people. Whether it be a child taking its first step, a student learning to add, a customer buying a tool, or an artist displaying a work of art, people need other people. The normal life span of the individual is a series of interactional exchanges between human beings. Laughing or crying, playing or working, buying or selling, dancing or dying—all these and innumerable other human activities have meaning only in relation to other people.

The fact that human beings are social animals serves as the basis for sociology. Sociologists study groups. They want to know what the groups are, how they are organized, how people interact within them, how groups affect individuals, and how individuals affect groups.

In a sense, we are all sociologists. Children begin very early to justify their behavior by the retort, "Well, everyone else is doing it." That statement may be translated, "I have observed my reference group (the people whose life-style I seek to imitate) and found that this specific behavior is acceptable to them. Therefore, I want to do it." Or, one sometimes hears the statement, "Children from low income areas have a difficult time in school because they do not come from a home conducive to learning." This line of argument goes on to point out the lack of parental encouragement as well as the paucity of role models that the child may imitate. It is a sociological

1

argument based upon the impact of the group (in this case, the child's family and community) upon the individual's behavior.

Popular proverbs sometimes include sociological thinking. For example, consider these "old sayings": "Birds of a feather flock together." "One bad apple can ruin a barrel." "Families that pray together, stay together." Whether there is truth to the statements or not, they show the popular understanding that there is a connection between group life and individual behavior.

When we ask for averages or statistics that deal with human behavior, we are seeking sociological information. What was the average family income in the United States in 1960? Was it more or less in 1970? How many people move to California each month? How many families in New York City earn less than $6,000 per year? What percentage of blacks voted in the presidential election in 1976? What is the current unemployment rate? The answers to these questions, which are of interest to all of us, are aspects of group life associated with our society. They are sociological questions because they measure human activity in groups.

Thus, people think sociologically in everyday life. Let us now look at how the professional sociologist looks at these phenomena.

The Task of Sociology

Sociology as a discipline may be defined as the *scientific study of human behavior in a group context.* As such, no aspect of human interaction is exempt from its area of consideration. Demographers study population growth, rates of birth and death, and migration patterns. Criminologists consider the motives as well as the deeds of the criminal. Social rehabilitation, juvenile delinquency, legal changes, and penal institutions are among their areas of concern. Social psychologists study everything from human aggressiveness to motives and attitudes. There are urban sociologists, family sociologists, and community sociologists. In addition to these areas of concern, sociologists study stratification, race relations, religion, personality development, fads and fashion, war, old age, youth, sex, work, and recreation. More recently, specialties in the areas of sex roles, the future, and sociology of sports have appeared. It appears that no type of human behavior is overlooked by sociologists in their study of "the group context."

Sociology attempts to be scientific. The professional sociologist attempts to use the attitude and methods of science in the study of human behavior.

Science is the effort to acquire knowledge that conforms to empirical reality. It is a way of knowing and is based upon both reason and empirical evidence. The scientist uses logic or experience or intuition to set up a theory of how or why a specific phenomenon works. This theory, or set of ideas, is a rational explanation of that which the scientist assumes conforms to reality. Then, to test the theory, the scientist performs an experiment designed to determine if reality is as it was predicted.

For example, Professor Erlenmeyer, a scientist, may have reason to believe that mating among rats is impaired by overcrowding. He reasons that rats, when crowded into a small space for long periods of time, will exhibit deviant behavior. They will become aggressive and cannibalistic. The male-female ritual that precedes mating will become deterred under these conditions, and copulation will be infrequent. This oversimplified set of propositions, let us say, is his theory. He then designs an experiment and checks his theory against the actual conditions of life. His theory may be correct or incorrect. (In this case, the theory is correct.) Thus, scientific knowledge is acquired by asking the question, "Does what I predict correspond to observable data?"

Science stresses objectivity; that is, the scientist must attempt in every way to reduce his or her own biases. When one allows personal likes or dislikes, emotions, values, or attitudes to enter in, serious distortions in observations or analysis may occur. In the search for "truth," the scientist must not let her or his own wishes color the findings of research.

Thus, in the pursuit of the knowledge of social life, the rigid demands of the scientific method and attitude must be applied. In the effort to describe, explain, and predict human behavior in a group context, the sociologist's findings must conform to empirical evidence.

In fairness, however, you should be aware that sociologists (as other social scientists) labor under two significant limitations that the natural scientists (physicists, chemists, biologists) do not normally confront. The first is that the sociologist may not, in most circumstances, specifically design an experiment to test a theory. One does not manipulate people like one does rats, for example. One may deliberately infect mice with a certain virus to determine if cancer will result. But one may not do the same with human subjects. Social scientists are limited, normally, to ex post facto experimental designs. They must find people who, in the natural processes of life, have been subjected to the variable that is under consideration. Then they compare this group to a similar group not exposed to the variable. It is easy to see that such a method cannot successfully control all variables that may have had an impact on the subjects under study.

The second limitation that the sociologist confronts is equally as serious. The subject matter of sociology is human beings. These creatures bring to their behavior an ingredient not characteristic, so far as we know, of the subjects of the physical scientist. Humans invest their activity with meaning. The principles that affect rats in overcrowded conditions may or *may not* be the principles that affect humans under similar circumstances. People act, but they have a reason for it. One may determine the number of alcoholics in the United States with reasonable accuracy. But to determine what social forces are connected with the increasing amount of alcoholism in this society is a different matter. What values and attitudes of the society contribute to this situation? What meaning does the individual attribute to his or her behavior? What is the home condition and experience and/or work situation of the alcoholic? These and other important variables enter the research problem of the sociologist interested in this phenomenon.

Thus, the sociologist is a scientist who studies the behavior of people in groups by developing theories and testing these theories by observation and experimentation in real life. As a scientist, the sociologist seeks to build a field of knowledge based on the attitude and method of science that describes, explains, and predicts human behavior in a group context. How does she or he go about this task?

The Sociologist at Work

People are unique, but their behavior is patterned. For example, students in a classroom differ from one another, but they do many things alike. Their behavior is orderly and predictable because of the patterns established for appropriate classroom behavior. It is these similarities of behavior that the sociologist seeks to find and explain. To discover these patterns and to find underlying variables affecting them is to go a long way in understanding why people act as they do.

For example, one problem that has perplexed educators for a number of years is the causes of underachievement in school. Why do some children of normal intelligence fail in school? This is, of course, a complex question of many parts and no simple statement can adequately answer it. But a significant variable recently uncovered and given much attention is diet. Children who in early life have had a protein-deficient diet and who have come to school with empty stomachs do not perform as well as adequately fed children. This simple statement does not fully explain school failure. Diet is a part of a complex set of variables associated with school performance. But poor diet is *one* variable that is a part of the *pattern* of child behavior in school. In such bits and pieces, sociologists (and other scientists) go about studying and explaining human behavior.

How does one collect from real life the necessary data to test a theory? Here we are dealing with the question of methods. One must bridge the gap between one's ideas of reality (theory) and actual life. Crossing this chasm is by no means an easy task.

A number of methods have been devised by sociologists to collect the necessary information to test a theory. These methods include the following:

Mailed questionnaires—The investigator makes a list of questions that the informant is to answer and mails it to each selected respondent. The questions must be easily understood and able to be interpreted by the respondent as intended. Ambiguous questions lead to useless information. This method is a relatively inexpensive way to collect data from a large number of people. However, its greatest limitation is the possibility that large numbers of people may fail to return the questionnaire to the investigator.

Personal interview—As in the questionnaire method, a list of questions is drawn up. This list is called an *interview schedule,* and it is administered to respondents in a face-to-face situation in which the interviewer records the respondent's answers. This is probably a more effective method of collecting information than the questionnaire method. But, at the same time, it is also a more expensive and time-consuming method.

Case study—Sometimes it is desirable, depending on the nature of the study, to select relatively few individuals and collect information from each in depth. Usually a great deal more time is spent with each interviewee. One may even wish to use tapes and cameras to record behavior and opinions.

Observation—There may be times when asking questions is unnecessary or potentially disruptive of the behavior the sociologist wishes to record. In such a situation, he or she may simply observe the activity in an unobtrusive manner. One usually makes notes on the individuals in action (one may also film and/or tape the activity). Later some report is written on the observations.

Participant observation—If one desires to use this method, she or he adds participation to observation. One may simply sit in on an event to experience and observe it. Or one may live for a period of time among those he or she wishes to observe and record. The obvious advantage of such a method is that the sociologist becomes a part of the activity he or she is studying. Thus, one experiences the phenomenon "from the inside." The greatest danger in such an approach is the subjectivity and bias that may occur.

Use of available data — The sociologist must constantly be aware of data that are already collected in one form or another. Many federal, state, and local state agencies collect statistics useful to the social researcher. One obvious example is the Census Bureau. Histories, personal letters, biographies, and industrial statistics are other forms of available data that may be useful to the sociologist.

Sociology and Social Problems

Much sociological research deals with phenomena generally regarded as "social problems." Alcoholism, sex offenses, juvenile delinquency, divorce, drug addiction, and mental health are among the topics with which sociologists deal. What role does sociology play in "social solutions"? If the task of the sociologist is to discover and interpret facts about social life, including problems that inflict misery upon untold numbers of people, does this responsibility include solving these very problems?

The question of social reform is a thorny one and advocates on both sides are strong and vocal. The problem lies in two complex areas: (1) Does a problem exist and whose problem is it? (2) How do we go about solving the problem? Answers to these two questions are a reflection of the values of the people offering the solution. For example, is the answer to drug addiction stronger laws and tougher legislation? Or, is it to legalize addiction and open more methadone centers? Or, is it both? Or, as another example, do stronger laws and more stringent punishment of offenders, including capital punishment, deter crime? Or, do we need more attention given to prevention of crime and rehabilitation of the criminal? When sociologists venture into these and related areas, do they lose their objectivity? Yet, if they do not offer opinions on these issues, where are there more qualified people to do so?

Perhaps the answer to the sociologists' dilemma lies in following a middle-road position. They must make certain that social research reflects the highest possible scientific standards. The scientific mandate to objectivity and test by empirical evidence belongs to the sociologist no less than the atomic scientist. Sociological conclusions must be bound by the rigor of these limitations. When sociologists venture beyond that point, their opinions on solving problems and social reform must be labeled as just that — opinions.

The Beginnings of Sociology

The word *sociology* was coined in 1839 by a Frenchman named Auguste Comte. He and others during this time were concerned with the social disorder that plagued their society following the French Revolution and Napoleonic era in Europe. Comte, particularly, was interested in the concept of social order. What factors contributed to the maintenance of society? That is, what held society together? Comte called this factor *social statics*. On the other hand, how did society change? (This Comte referred to as *social dynamics*.) The study of natural phenomena had ushered in disciplines such as chemistry, biology, astronomy, and physics, and Comte was familiar with these sciences. He suggested that the methods and approaches developed in these areas be applied to the subject of society. The new science, Comte said, would be called sociology. Comte continued until his death in 1857 to lecture and write about this new discipline.

His suggestions bore fruit. Other Frenchmen followed his concepts and further refined them. Gabriel Tarde studied family structure and criminal behavior. Gustave Le Bon looked at crowd behavior. Emile Durkheim studied suicide rates, religion, and social cohesion.

By the late nineteenth century people from other countries were contributing to the development of sociology. Vilfredo Pareto, a Frenchman reared in Italy, described society as a system (like in physics). The first sociology course in America was taught in 1872 at Yale by a minister named William Graham Sumner. In Germany Max Weber and in England a German Jew named Karl Marx were writing about economic variables and social life. The first graduate school of sociology in the world was started in 1892 at the University of Chicago by Albion Small. In 1895 Small founded *The American Journal of Sociology* and with George E. Vincent produced the first textbook in sociology, *An Introduction to the Study of Society.*

Today sociology enjoys enthusiastic and widespread acceptance. As an academic discipline, it may be studied in almost any college and university in the United States and Canada. Most European and South American countries, as well as Eastern and Middle Eastern nations, have a number of universities where sociology is taught. And since 1950 the *International Sociological Association* has met at regular intervals. There is also an International Rural Sociological Society. There are a number of national associations like The American Sociological Association, and in the United States regional associations are very popular.

Summary

Sociology may be defined as the scientific study of human behavior in a group context. The sociologist seeks to describe, explain, and predict human behavior in interactional situations. The scientific attitude of objectivity as well as the scientific method of experimentation and observation are important to the sociologist. One's theory must be corroborated by reality, and thus sociological knowledge is built. Sociologists use mailed questionnaires, personal interview, case study, observation, participant observation, and available data as methods of collecting information by which theories are tested.

From its beginning in the early nineteenth century, sociology has grown in its precision of investigation as well as its popularity. Today it boasts an international character and may be studied in universities the world over.

Additional Readings

Barnes, Harry Elmer. *An Introduction to the History of Sociology,* abridged ed. Chicago: University of Chicago Press, 1966.

Berger, Peter L. *Invitation to Sociology: A Humanistic Perspective.* New York: Doubleday and Co., 1963.

Calhoun, Donald W. *Persons-In-Groups: A Humanistic Social Psychology.* New York: Harper and Row, 1976.

Homans, George C. *The Human Group.* New York: Harcourt and Brace, 1950.

Kitchens, James A., and Estrada, Leobardo F. *Individuals in Society: A Modern Introduction to Sociology.* Columbus, Ohio: Charles E. Merrill Publishing Co., 1974.

Mills, C. Wright. *The Sociological Imagination.* New York: Oxford University Press, 1959.

Turner, Jonathan H. *The Structure of Sociological Theory.* Homewood, Ill.: Dorsey Press, 1978.

two

Sociology and the Social Structure

Few people reading these words have not experienced firsthand the confusion, discouragement, and exhaustion associated with college registration. Most colleges and universities register large numbers of people in relatively brief time periods, and the resultant crowding and congestion, to say nothing of the endless lines, is an amazing testimony to human tenacity and patience. Yet, despite the inevitable mistakes and short tempers, it all seems to come out right and students and teachers end up at the right place at the right time on the first day of class. How does order result from such apparent chaos? Sociologists answer this question by referring to the concept of social structure.

Social structure is another way of speaking of organization in society. It is the principle that gives a society, or a group in society, a shape or form. Just as materials are shaped by the sculptor into a form, and thereby shapeless clay becomes an image, so society is formed, or organized into a structure. In such a manner, people are allowed to interact in an orderly fashion and to accomplish both individual and collective goals.

Let's return to that group of students and professors on the first day of class. Forty-five individuals assemble in a given room of a specified building at a few minutes before nine in the morning. They are all strangers. At precisely nine o'clock a bell rings and one person in the group calls for attention. The others become quiet and listen. At given intervals those seated write down in their notebooks statements that this person makes. One of those seated wishes to speak. He raises his hand above his head, is recognized by the person to whom all have been listening, and makes his statement. For an hour this arrangement continues until again the bell sounds. Those seated close their notebooks and file out of the room. The lecturer follows. What has allowed this group of strangers in new surroundings to interact in this orderly and, hopefully, educational manner? Again, the sociologist refers to social structure.

Human social behavior is not random. It is structural. A group of children playing sandlot baseball do not act like the same group of children learning to tie knots or start a campfire in a scout troop. The same children would behave differently in a Sunday school class and still differently at a birthday party. Each social setting has a different "look" because of its structure. The carpenter saws and nails to give lumber the shape (or structure) of a stereo cabinet. Its form distinguishes it from a coffee table or a chair. Both society and groups within a society have structure, and the result is both orderly and predictable behavior.

In such a manner people are able to live, work, play, and communicate in groups. Just as stoplights and a few simple rules of driving allow hundreds of motorists to move tons of steel and human bodies through city streets at peak traffic hours, so the structure of groups allows people to interact meaningfully and "get where they are going." Without it, group activity would be paralyzed.

The Basic Elements of Social Structure

At least three elements must be clearly perceived if one is to understand how social structure works. These three elements are *norms, roles,* and *positions.* They are the keys to comprehending group activity.

Norms

Norms may be defined simply as *shared behavioral expectations.* They are the rules of appropriate behavior shared by those people interacting, and they are a part of virtually every human exchange. They tell us how we are to act and, since they are shared, we know that others expect us to act in this approved manner. Have you ever been in a nice restaurant and ordered a T-bone steak? In polite company one cuts the steak with a knife (one piece at a time) and eats it with a fork. You have probably noticed the meat left on the bone. Why not pick it up with your hands and eat the meat remaining? Because there are shared behavioral expectations that inhibit this behavior.

William Graham Sumner, in his book *Folkways* published in 1908, first drew our attention in a systematic manner to norms and their impact on behavior. Sumner divided norms into three categories: *folkways, mores,* and *laws.*

Folkways are the lowest level of norms and are little more than polite or courteous customs. They are easily, and often, broken and bear little or no punishment for the offender since they are not necessary for individual or social survival. Saying "excuse me" after one sneezes, not burping in public, or not staring at another in public are examples of folkways. Other folkways of a slightly more serious nature are the prohibition of racial slurs, the use of certain four-letter words, (or other obscenities in specified settings), and of touching various parts of one's anatomy in public.

Mores, on the other hand, carry more saliency or importance because they are concerned with individual or social survival. These rules, therefore, bear more punishment for the offender when broken. A student, for example, who disrupts class with loud, offensive talk will likely be negatively sanctioned (punished) by the instructor or other classmates. "Brown nosing," i.e., the activity of attempting to ingratiate oneself to a superior, may likewise be met with negative sanctions. A significant *mos* (singular of mores) in our society is the right to a space (e.g., seat on a bus) to the individual first occupying it.

When mores are raised to official codification they become laws. Official bodies like legislatures or Congress enact laws. Usually, though not always as we shall see, they are the most functional mores and are necessary for both individual and group survival. Offenders are rather severely punished for breaking them. Official bodies such as courts are designed to evaluate a person's guilt or innocence with regard to these norms. Punishment varies from small fines to imprisonment or in some cases even forfeiture of the offender's life. An attempt is usually made to make the punishment "fit" the functionality of the law. For example, traffic fines are usually small for "minor" offenses such as speeding. But large fines or imprisonment are levied against an individual judged guilty of causing serious injury or death due to negligent driving.

Some laws, enacted in the past and remaining on the law books, have lost their functionality in present society. One example might be the so-called "blue laws." These laws prohibit, in some states, selling certain merchandise on Sunday. These laws originated in New England during colonial times, and their name (*blue laws)* stems from the color of paper on which they were printed. In states where these laws have not been repealed, stores are allowed to sell certain goods, e.g., groceries, but may not sell other merchandise, such as shoes or furniture, on Sunday.

The functionality of other laws is immediately obvious. Prohibitions of murder, stealing, and the necessity of honoring legal contracts, such as paying bills, are necessary if our modern, economically oriented, and mass society is to continue. Laws that govern economic factors in our society are the most numerous and the most stringently punished when broken.

Norms, then, are rules of appropriate or acceptable behavior. They provide for stable and orderly arrangements among groups of interacting individuals. They keep individuals from having to undergo the problems of enacting rules in each new situation and make orderly transition from one generation to the next.

Norms, however, do change or else society would be most boring and sterile. Some norms are made to be broken. For example, rules governing fashions last for but a season and then are altered, sometimes drastically. Also, subcultural and regional differences in expected behavior are significant in changing norms. Rules for appropriate behavior in a Northern, urban ghetto may be different from those in a Southern girl's school. Geographical mobility and the mass media expose the normal American citizen to these heterogeneous and changing bodies of normative structure. In such a manner, existing standards for behavior are called into question and sometimes disregarded. Finally, norms are altered by simple deviance. Well-established standards are broken deliberately and knowingly. The result is a change in the norms. Two examples come immediately to mind. First, fifty years ago (or even less in some places) it was considered repugnant for women to smoke in public. But women followed the example of men and smoked in public. Without a doubt, many female reputations were tarnished by this blatant act of defiance and deviance. In the intervening years, female smoking has become acceptable as norms have been changed to redefine this act. Second, the Civil Rights Movement in the late fifties and early sixties was based upon the simple conviction that some legal norms were unjust. Early nonviolent advocates such as Martin Luther King, Jr., and his followers deliberately broke these laws. They willingly accepted the legal, and frequently illegal, punishment associated with the laws in order to reveal the injustice of the law. In such a manner they hoped to prevail upon the good conscience of the American public and thus remove unjustly restrictive laws. They succeeded, and some laws were declared unconstitutional and were replaced by laws upholding constitutionally guaranteed equality. Additionally, many mores affecting relationships between the races have been altered to include more healthy and positive interchange.

Roles

In theatrical usage, the word *role* denotes a character in a script that an individual portrays as part of a play. The role requires words to be spoken, gestures to be made, and costumes to be worn. In short one's role in a play is the composite of his or her activity in the play. The role identifies the actor and gives him or her certain rights and obligations in the play.

The theatrical use of the word *role* is not far from its sociological use. In real life, however, an individual plays numerous roles. One moves, so to speak, from one play to another in life. The acceptance of a role, in sociological terms, means that an individual accepts a given set of norms as applicable to his or her behavior. Thus, for the sociologist, a role may be defined as a cluster or set of norms that governs a person's action in a given situation or in the performance of a given function.

Perhaps an illustration might help clarify the sociological concept of role. Think about the traditional concept of fatherhood. For years to be a father in American society meant that an individual carried out specific functions. Among these functions have been the following: the provider or breadwinner, the disciplinarian, and a vocational guide or teacher of his children. Each of these functions has carried a set or cluster, of behavioral expectations or norms. Each of these sets of norms has been a role that the father has played in his family. The provider role has implied that he would be gainfully employed and that he would use his income to provide for the needs of his family. Each role has dictated how a man would perform his part in the "play" of family living. Together they would determine the rights and obligations of his "part" in fatherhood.

Being a father in American society has, of course, changed in some respects as the norms have changed. Many young men entering marriage are not as sure today as were their grandfathers what is expected of them as fathers. Is one to be *the* breadwinner or is the provider role to be more equally shared? Fathers today send their children to school for vocational guidance. Boys and girls no longer work alongside parents to learn vocational or technical skills. New norms guide behavior in this area. Contemporary fathers perform their various roles in the play differently

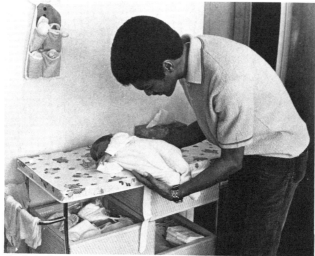

The parental role is changing.

than did those of preceding generations. The words to be spoken, the gestures to be made, and the costumes to be worn are different because the script has been changed and roles altered.

Positions

The term *position* (or *status position* as it is sometimes called) describes for the sociologist all the roles a person plays in a given group of which he or she is a part. Thus, a position is a cluster of roles. In our preceding illustration of fatherhood, the technical term denoting the father's position is *Husband Father*. In precise sociological usage an individual has only one position in each group in which he or she interacts. In class you may be a student. This is your position. It in turn is made up of the roles you play in that group. They may range from notetaker to test taker to friend. The rights and obligations of each role accrue to you by virtue of your position as student. Each role is in turn a body of norms that guides your behavior while you perform your role.

When you leave class you may attend a meeting of the student council as representative of your sorority, fraternity, or other organization. In this group you assume a specific position that is a cluster of the roles you play in that group. That evening, let us say, you return to your dorm where again you assume a specific position. In such a manner you move from position to position as you go from one group to another. The content of each position is made up of a cluster of roles and these in turn are made up of sets of norms.

Human Interaction

The essence of human social life is interaction. People meet and carry out transactions or exchanges of every conceivable type. We need and therefore depend upon each other, and the expression of these needs is found in the countless interactions of individuals and groups that make up a society. Interaction, broadly defined, is two or more people taking each other into account in their behavior. In an interactional situation one person is aware of and therefore is acting on the basis of the other person. Let us say that two acquaintances meet on the sidewalk as they make their way to work in the morning. They exchange pleasantries, which might include smiles, nods, or the wave of a hand. They might say such things as, "How are you today?" or "Have a nice day today." In this brief sidewalk exchange each person's behavior is based upon the presence and actions of the other. Had the other not been present, each, no doubt, would not have acted as he did. Or, as in our earlier example, the professor enters at the stroke of nine and begins to lecture. As he or she does, students take notes and ask questions or make comments. Both professor and students are taking each other into account in their behavior.

Interaction is facilitated by the simple fact that individuals can *predict* the behavior of others. And predictability, in turn, is based upon the basic elements of social structure. Shared behavioral expectations (norms) that are combined into roles and positions give a "structure" to behavior. Thus one knows what to expect in general terms from other people in interactional situations. As a teacher I know what to expect from students even prior to the first day of class. And they in turn know what they may expect in general from me.

What this means is that individuals entering interactional situations do not have to waste time coming to agreements concerning how the interaction is to be carried out. Where roles and norms exist, ready-made expectations serve as a guide to behavior. When, for example, two people get married, many rights and obligations accrue to them as they take on the positions of husband and wife. Such a statement is not intended to deny that many adjustments must be made nor to deny that each person does not have to learn what the other expects. In our society, based as it is upon heterogeneous groups with varying expectations and characterized by changing, transient norms, each couple must of necessity work out many rules for behavior. But two people entering marriage have the comfort of knowing that many behaviors are undergirded by socially approved norms. The exception rather than the rule would be the couple who enters marriage with no preconceived ideas of what it means to be a "husband" or a "wife."

Interaction, then, is predictable and orderly because a society or subculture provides a general framework for behavior of individuals. Without this framework social behavior would be random and chaotic because no one would know what to expect either from himself or herself or from others.

Thinkers in this area, however, point out that if interactional encounters were limited to these prescribed areas, society would indeed be a sterile place. There are shared behavioral expectations for the position of teacher, but not all teachers are alike. The word *husband* or *wife* has a meaning derived in part from the rights and obligations associated with that social position. But not all husbands or wives are alike. How do these thinkers account for these obvious and well-known differences? They point out that social positions are made up of three types of roles: prescribed, subjective, and enacted.

The *prescribed role* is the ideal. It consists of the general and broad expectations that are a part of the position. Teachers are expected, for example, to be fair, knowledgeable about their subject matter, relatively courteous, and accessible.

Students, on the other hand, are expected to be somewhat intellectually curious, attentive, teachable, and consistent in attendance and study habits.

The *subjective role* allows for individual differences in interpreting the prescribed role. Personality factors, the actual situation, and the strength of social pressures are factors that allow the individual leeway in applying the ideal to oneself. Some teachers are more friendly with students and may therefore be more accessible than other teachers. One person's personality may make it more difficult to interact with ease in teacher/student relationships than would be true of another.

Finally, the *enacted role* is the individual's actual behavior. A given teacher is not absolutely consistent in his or her behavior. One may be more at ease with undergraduate classes than with graduate classes. Or, on one day the individual may be rather curt because of income tax problems or a hangover. On another day, the same person may be relaxed, jovial, and friendly.

Interaction is orderly and predictable because society provides a general framework of norms, roles, and positions within which behavior takes place. Room is left in these basic elements of social structure for individual interpretations and situational factors to have impact on the interactional exchange. Our question now becomes, "How is this general framework dispersed to the people that make up society?"

Socialization

One significant difference between human beings and other primates (the great apes, chimpanzees, and monkeys) is the human capacity to think symbolically or abstractly. Humans, in this regard, seem to have a facility that is either absent or present in only a limited degree in other primates. The capacity for abstract thought results in at least three distinct advantages of people over monkeys. First, humans can conceive a visual image and "imprint" that image on available materials and other matter to construct objects useful for life. This means that humans are "toolmakers." Humans, therefore, help to create the environment they live in. Primates, of course, utilize available materials in toollike fashion. Chimps, for example, take small branches and, after stripping off the leaves, poke them into ant hills. The ants attack the intruding stick, cling to it, and are lifted from their earthly home to become a delicious morsel for the chimp's palate. But no chimp ever cultivates a bed of ants or practices the tactics of animal (or ant) husbandry to grow bigger and better ants. Nor does a chimp use electronic equipment to dig the ants from the earth or freezers to preserve them for future cooking needs. Only humans do that. Chimps manipulate their environment, but humans create it.

Second, human beings' symbolizing brains allows them to "take themselves as an object." That is, humans have the ability to be self-transcendent. They can stand outside themselves and view their own behavior. Thus, one is able to say, "Boy, I gave a good speech," or "That was a beautiful touchdown pass I threw." Humans, because of this capacity, have a self-image and that factor will become important when we discuss personality development in the next section.

Third, humans depend less upon innate biological predisposition (instincts) for behavior than any other animal. In the evolutionary development of Homo sapiens, instincts became less important in favor of human learning capacity based upon the increasingly large and more complex brain.

Experiments have shown that subhuman primates must undergo a period in early life when they learn the skills necessary to live as one of their species. Young monkeys, deprived of this learning process, cannot cope with their natural habitat. Monkeys reared in isolation from other monkeys, it seems, never adjust to monkey-dom. This process takes longer among humans than any other species. It appears also that this process is *absolutely* necessary for humans since all social behavior is based upon learning and nothing is left to instincts. This learning process is called *socialization.*

Socialization may be defined as the procedure by which the individual is taught the skills, attitudes, and values necessary for proper participation in his or her society. The socialization process begins very early in life. A child is categorized according to sex almost immediately after birth by her or his name. This is a permanent status ascription and much learning will take place in the child's early life to insure that he or she identifies with the proper sex. From that early age, the child is confronted with an almost endless list of things that he or she is or is not to do.

Incidental, as well as purposeful, statements from parents, teachers, older siblings, playmates, and others help to form impressions of proper conduct. Mothers say "One doesn't take toys that belong to others." Or they say, "Be sure and study your spelling work; you don't want to fail." Or, "Comb your hair so that you can look your best." In such a manner, the child learns the skills, values, and attitudes that allow him or her to live successfully in American society.

Socialization is a lifelong process. As one advances from one stage of life to another, new behaviors are expected, and they must be learned. Two terms are important at this point: *desocialization* and *anticipatory socialization.*

Desocialization is the process of unlearning behaviors that were acceptable at earlier stages of life. New armed services recruits are sometimes stunned by "boot camp." Many of the harshest aspects of these first few weeks of military service are based upon the necessity of "unlearning" habits acquired as adolescent civilians. Abrupt methods are sometimes used to facilitate this desocialization process. Some-times an individual's initial foray into the occupational world is accompanied by the same jolting desocialization process. Indeed, almost any time an individual moves into a new social position, some desocialization is necessary.

Anticipatory socialization, on the other hand, refers to learning about expected behavior prior to entering a new social position. High school students, looking forward to their own college experiences, often ask friends or relatives who are in college, "What's it like to go to college?" Anticipatory socialization occurs when that question is answered. All stages of the life cycle from very early years to old age are frequented by anticipatory socizliation.

Society eases the socialization process by providing individuals with what may be called *agents of socialization.* In general, these agents may fall into five categories.

The Family

Of primary importance in socializing the individual to social life is the family. Here each person has his or her first contact with social arrangements. Everything from toilet training to aggression control to proper pronunciation of simple words takes on significance in the family. Because these experiences come first in life, because the individual is so dependent for physical and social survival upon these people, and because the individual is so impressionistic at this early age, these socialization experiences are of primary importance in the individual's social development.

The School

Schools teach the individuals more than the three Rs. They impart very significant values for the individual's participation in society. Schools teach people the value of ambition, competition, obedience, diligence, conformity, individuality, patriotism, law and order, romance, and other salient elements of American character. Occupational skills are also learned in school.

Peer Groups

For youngsters, but no less so for adults, friendship cliques of one's own sex and age are important agents of socialization. These groups for adolescents form a transition between the family on the one hand and the community on the other. They authenticate the "in" thing and are based almost completely on the value of conformity (to the norms of the peer group). Not infrequently, peer groups promote deviance from the rules of both the family and the community by encouraging "taboo" behavior and discussion of forbidden subjects. They are important in communicating subcultural skills, attitudes, and values.

The Mass Media

Television, movies, radio, newspapers, and magazines are highly significant agents of socialization in our mass, urban society. One cogent proof of their effect in shaping behavior is the billions of advertising dollars spent annually to create demand for the products of mass production. The media not only entertain us and help us pass the hours away, but they sell us things. In so doing, they help to shape our values and attitudes as well as direct our behavior. Consider as a single example mouthwash commercials on TV. Most frequently, the users of these commodities are young people who are bright and attractive. They use a mouthwash to enhance romance, to get a raise in salary, or to get an occupational promotion. What values undergird these pitches? Achievement and competition. The logic of the commercial is, don't let someone else beat you by taking your girl, getting a higher salary, or advancing occupationally more rapidly than you.

The Church

Religious mores (or morals as they are most frequently called) are a part of the normative structure of society. That is, moral prescriptions are themselves norms because they fit our definition of shared behavioral expectations. Our society's emphasis on honesty (not cheating in school, honoring a contract, paying one's bills) grew naturally out of the religious commandment, "Thou shalt not steal." Marital fidelity is associated with the prohibition against adultery, and laws against murder are supported by the commandment, "Thou shalt not kill."

But churches teach more than religious norms. They, like schools, also communicate values and attitudes that support the total society. Sermons, hymns, liturgies,

*Various agents ease the
socialization process.*

and religious holidays sometimes underscore things like patriotism, consumerism, progress, and growth in a secular sense. These latter values of progress and growth may be seen in the church's implied assertion that massive buildings, increasing budgets, growing membership rolls, and comfortable pews are evidence of God's blessings.

The importance of the religious institution should not be seen as limited to people who attend church. Agents such as the school and the family also impart religious norms. Also, the church has made use of the mass media. Radio ministers, televised church services, and even billboards advertise the presence and message of the church. (Who, for example, has not seen somewhere painted on a large rock or the side of a building the words *Jesus saves?*)

Individuals have the opportunity, then, to learn those things necessary to make it in society by their constant contact with these agents of socialization. Sometimes, and this is especially true in a mass, heterogeneous society, messages to the individual from these agents may be in conflict. For example, the family may teach some expectations that are at variance with that which the individual hears at church. Or, the peer group may challenge what the school and the family is communicating to the individual. For example, one may hear at church that one is to love others and help those who are in need. At home, however, one may hear and even see intolerance and unforgiveness set forth as prime virtues. Without a doubt, such conflicting socialization contributes to the ambiguity of norms. Individuals are caught in a marginal position and in some cases never resolve the conflict between the mutually exclusive expectations.

You should also be aware at this point that the content of the socialization process in our society may vary from one region and subculture of the country to another. The skills, attitudes, and values conveyed to individuals in low-income, Northern, urban areas may have little in common with those in a white, upper-class, suburban area of the South. But the point is that, while different in content, individuals in both settings are served by these agents of socialization in their area of subculture and have opportunity to learn the structure necessary to make it in their segment of the society.

How? In what manner does the individual "take in" the content of this socialization process? This question leads us to our next topic of consideration—personality development.

Personality Development

Human beings are much the same at the beginning of life. They are infant primates rather incapable of any meaningful activity and totally dependent upon others for physical sustenance. They differ in two important ways: (1) each carries a predetermined genetic makeup that affects such things as potential physical build and intelligence and (2) each is born into a specific social environment that will shape that infant into a living, thinking, and acting human being. From the interplay of these two factors emerges what is usually referred to as one's "personality."

Personality may be defined as the probability that an individual will act a certain way in a certain situation. Thus, personality is a characteristic way of behaving.

Individual personalities are unique because individuals react to stimuli in various ways. Your usual or most frequent response to a certain set of stimuli is your personality. You may be quiet and shy in groups. Or, you may be the life of the party. You may display excessive temper when confronted with situations that displease you. On the other hand, you may be dependable and steady in crisis situations. You may lean more to serious, hard work than lackadaisical, nonchalant behavior. The word *personality* for the sociologist is, then, a term that characterizes an individual's usual response to a given situation.

Biologically determined factors are of significance in the process of personality development. Genetic makeup is important in setting outer limits (or potential) for certain types of growth. Consider, as examples, intelligence and athletic ability. Both factors are valued in American society. One's biological makeup helps to determine one's potential capacity in each area. The ability to learn is an inherited capacity to a great extent. The upper reaches of IQ are set by genetic characteristics. The potential may never be reached, of course, because of environmental conditions. But individuals with innate capacity to learn effectively and quickly are at a decided advantage in American society. They are likely to be more highly rewarded, especially in school. In the same vein, athletic ability is affected by genetic characteristics. While the ability to run a hundred yards in nine seconds must be developed, the capacity to do so is innate. One born with this potential is fortunate indeed in our society when it is developed and comes to the attention of an athletic coach.

The point is that one's genes determine much of one's physical capacities and physical build. Certain types of physical capacities and build are more valued in our society. Those individuals who possess, by virtue of their genetic combination, these characteristics will probably be more rewarded in their interpersonal relationships.

But of greater importance, according to the sociological tradition, in the process of personality development is the nature and quality of one's social environment. Interaction creates what sociologists call the *social self.* Personality is dependent upon the individual's self-image or social self.

The Looking Glass Self

Around the turn of the century, Charles Horton Cooley introduced into sociology the term *looking glass self*. He used the term to describe the process of developing a self-image or social self.[1]

According to Cooley, the most important human interaction takes place in *primary groups*. These groups are characterized by affection, warmth, intimacy, friendship, and sentiment. (*Secondary groups,* a term not used by Cooley, would typically be made up of impersonal, legal, and utilitarian relationships.) Interaction in the context of primary groups forms the basis of one's self-image. The group serves as a mirror, or looking glass, in which the individual perceives himself or herself. Three steps occur in this process: (1) the individual imagines his or her appearance (the impact of one's behavior, dress, speech, etc.) upon other people; (2) the individual imagines the evaluation of others concerning that appearance; (3) the individual experiences some form of self-feeling, such as pride, satisfaction, shame, embarrassment, security, or anxiety.

Through this process the individual develops a self-concept or way of viewing himself or herself, and positive or negative self-feelings occur. It is important to note that all this goes on inside the individual. One *imagines* how others are evaluating him or her. It is this perception and not the actual evaluation of others that creates the self-image. One's perceptions of the situation may or may not be correct.

Significant Others and the Generalized Other

About thirty years after Cooley, George Herbert Mead added to our understanding of the social self by introducing the ideas of *significant others* and the development of the *generalized other*.[2] Mead emphasized that we communicate through meaningful symbols. We use gestures and words to convey meaning in interactional situations. We learn the meaning of these symbols from our social environment. Children learn that it is "good" to be "big boys or girls." (Note in connection with our earlier discussion that the term *big boy* or *big girl* is a childhood "role.") They also learn that "big boys and girls" do not wet their pants. Rather, they "wee-wee" in the "potty" (a norm for the role of big boy or girl). Parents smile when a child obeys the norm and frown when he or she does not. In such a manner, a *meaningful* interaction is learned by the child.

Parents and other members of primary groups are "significant others" according to Mead. These people convey to the growing child both the symbols and their meaning. The growing child internalizes (or learns) what these people teach. For example, most parents (and other significant others in the child's early life) attempt to teach the child that unbridled aggression is to be avoided. A parent will say, "You mustn't bite your sister," or may even spank the child's hand. At this early stage of development, the physical presence of the parent is necessary to restrain the child from aggressive acts. To the extent that the parent is successful, the maturing child will resist the temptation to aggression because it will displease the parent. At this developmental stage, the actual thought of the parent deters the child. Later in life, perhaps in adolescence, the individual has so internalized this concept that unbridled aggression is not his or her "nature." That is, he or she does not like to fight. The individual prefers to negotiate rather than resort to aggressive acts. When this occurs, the significant others have become the generalized other. That is, the community has replaced the parent as the child has taken into his or her "personality" this aspect of the cultural surroundings. Aggression is redirected into more socially acceptable channels and the young adult's self-image or social self does not include biting a sibling.

Reference Groups

Interactional exchanges continue to play a part even in adult self-image development. It is true, of course, that one's basic personality and self-concept are developed early in life. But these can and do continue to change in various ways and in varying degrees. One powerful influence on these changes is called, by sociologists, *reference groups.*

A reference group may be defined as the group whose standards one seeks to emulate. Another way of saying the same thing is that reference groups are those whose norms one is willing to obey. The term was coined in 1942 by H. H. Hyman in a study on socioeconomic status.[3] Each person thinks of himself or herself as belonging to a certain social class dependent upon what social groups are used as a framework of judgment. Thus, according to Hyman, the term *reference group* refers to the group one uses as a basis for self-appraisal. These groups may be organized along economic, educational, religious, ethnic, or cultural lines. Or, they may be a combination of these factors.

Later work in this area has been done by Robert K. Merton and Alice S. Kitt.[4] In general, they note that reference groups serve to give individuals a sense of social solidarity by offering common values and shared expectations. The individual feels a sense of obligation to fulfill the normative standards put forward by the group. Reference groups "filter" the influence of the greater society as the individual interprets cultural demands of the larger social environment by reference to those with whom he or she interacts daily.

You should be aware of at least two further facts about reference groups. In the first place, American society is a mobile society in which individuals move both socially and geographically. Reference groups change and a person may, in fact, employ a variety of groups at different times. The particular group that serves this purpose at any given time is dependent upon a number of factors, such as the situation of the individual and the specific facet of behavior being evaluated.

In the second place, *reference individuals* (also called *role models*) are as important as reference groups. The individual identifying himself or herself with a reference person seeks to emulate the behavior and values of that individual. In some cases, the reference individual affects the behavior of the person in a very narrow context. In others, the influence is more general in its effect. For example, a young man may grow a beard because a certain rock singer has grown one. On the other hand, the same young man may seek to emulate the entire life-style of that singer as he understands it.

Social Structure and Personality

This chapter began with the assertion that a society is stable because of the existence of norms, roles, and positions that exist within it and that these elements are passed from one generation to another. Behavior is orderly and predictable because we share together certain behavioral expectations, values, and attitudes. Individuals may interact meaningfully because this general framework of behavior exists. But individuals do not go through a logical process of determining proper or appropriate behavior prior to each act of the day. They simply live. How then do these normative expectations get translated into behavior? The answer is through personality. As noted, the individual inculcates or ingests these expectations into his or her personality. Through the process of socialization and the resultant development of a social self or self-image, the society insures that individuals internalize the appropriate behavior in given situations. Normal individuals react in given situations that to them are an act of free will because they act from what is natural to them. They "express their personality."

Summary

Human behavior is not random; it is structured. Individuals in a society act in orderly and predictable ways so that both individual and social goals are accomplished. To insure this order and stability, each society is made up of norms, roles, and social positions. These basic elements of social structure insure smooth exchange between individuals and groups in a society. Individuals in society know in general what they may expect from people occupying specific positions in social groups. Interaction is facilitated because a society provides a general framework for the behavior of individuals.

The content of these behavioral expectations is communicated in society by the process of socialization. This process is most significant in the early, developing years of a person's life, but continues through all of life. At certain stages, individuals experience desocialization; at other stages, they may experience anticipatory socialization. Our society is characterized by at least five major agents of socialization. They are the family, the school, peer groups, the mass media, and the church.

Individuals inculcate behavioral expectations into their personalities. Primary groups as well as significant others provide a kind of mirror in which the individual develops a sense of himself or herself. One imagines his or her appearance to others, as well as other's evaluation of that appearance. The result is a self-evaluation of a positive or negative content.

As the individual internalizes the expectations of the significant others, he or she develops a set of personal expectations. Thus, the individual takes into his or her personality specified aspects of the social environment.

Throughout life the individual selects important social groups. He or she seeks to emulate the standards and behavior of this group or individual in given situations.

Notes

1. Charles Horton Cooley, *Human Nature and the Social Order* (New York: Charles Scribner's Sons, 1902), p. 152.

2. George Herbert Mead, *Mind, Self, and Society* (Chicago; University of Chicago Press, 1934), p. 154.

3. H.H. Hyman, "The Psychology of Status," *Archives of Psychology* 269 (1942): 162-69.

4. R.K. Merton and Alice S. Kitt, "Contributions to the Theory of Reference Group Behavior," in *Continuities in Social Research: Studies in the Scope and Method of "The American Soldier,"* ed. R.K. Merton and P.F. Lazarsfeld (Glencoe, Ill.: Free Press, 1950).

Additional Readings

Aronson, Elliot. *The Social Animal.* San Francisco: W. H. Freeman and Co., 1972.

Banton, Michael. *Roles: An Introduction to the Study of Social Relations.* New York: Basic Books, 1965.

Berne, Eric. *Games People Play: The Psychology of Human Relationships.* New York: Grove Press, 1969.

Cooley, Charles Horton. *Human Nature and the Social Order.* New York: Charles Scribner's Sons, 1902.

Goffman, Erving. The Presentation of Self in Everyday Life. Garden City, N.Y.: Doubleday, 1959.

Homans, George C. *Social Behavior: Its Elementary Forms.* rev. ed. New York: Harcourt Brace Jovanovich, 1974.

Kephart, William M. *Extraordinary Groups: The Sociology of Unconventional Life Styles.* New York: St. Martin's Press, 1976.

Mead, George H. *Mind, Self, and Society,* ed. Charles W. Morris. The University of Chicago Press 1934.

Ofshe, Richard, ed. *The Sociology of the Possible.* Englewood Cliffs, N.J.: Prentice-Hall, 1970.

White, Leslie A. *The Science of Culture.* New York: Farrar, Straus and Giroux, 1949.

three

Sociology and Human Behavior

Sociologists seek to describe and explain how humans behave in a group. They want to know what impact people have on each other. What is the relationship that individuals have to their society or to segments of that society known as subcultures? How does poverty or affluence affect humans? Do ethnic backgrounds make any difference in their behavior and the attitudes and actions of others toward them? Why are some people more overtly aggressive than others? These and a host of other questions are of interest as sociologists pursue knowledge of human behavior.

This chapter will provide some answers that sociologists give to these questions. Specifically, four areas of human interaction will concern us in this chapter. They are human behavior in collectivities, stratification, race relations, and aggression. This list is by no means a complete survey of the important areas of sociological knowledge. Each area has been selected because it is illustrative of the content of sociological inquiry and because most people reading this little book are affected to a greater or lesser degree by all these areas of social life.

Collective Behavior

An average day for most people in this society includes many hours spent with other people. In some cases, there is direct interaction among individuals, like a family eating breakfast together. However, some activities in the presence of others involve little or no interaction. Individuals waiting in line at the bank or riding together on a bus or watching a movie together communicate little and influence each other only indirectly. Sometimes an individual is with large groups of people, such as at a football game, in which little interaction occurs but where the excitement of crowd behavior is a major influence. People, it seems, can "get together" in a number of different ways.

When people are together but little direct interaction is occurring, they are involved in what sociologists call *collective behavior*. A *collectivity* may be defined as a relatively large number of people who have been exposed to a common stimulus and have responded to it with a minimum of communication or interaction. The collective behavior of people and people's influence upon each other is one of the most interesting areas of sociological study.

Sociologists study collective behavior of a number of different types. The first we may call *aggregates*. An aggregate is an assembly of people such as an audience, congregation, or a crowd. People watching a football game, listening to a symphony, attending religious services, Christmas shopping, or fleeing before a storm are an aggregate. A second type of collective behavior that the sociologist analyzes may be called *categories*. Collective behavior at this point does not even include physical proximity between individuals. Individuals are grouped (or categorized) for study according to some common characteristic they happen to share. Categories include such characteristics as education, income, age, or some behavioral element (e.g., delinquency). The third type of collective behavior that sociologists study is called *fads and fashions*. The focal point here is some human behavior that, for no apparent reason, "catches on" and captivates a large number of people for either a very brief or somewhat more extended period. The activity may involve toys like hula-hoops or C.B. radios. Or, it may be a somewhat more serious activity like the popularity of Eastern philosophies, religion, or transcendental meditation.

An audience is an example of an aggregate.

In general, collective behavior is episodic. That is, in most cases individuals do not congregate routinely or with regularity into collectivities. The common stimulus to which they are collectively responding brings them together. They unite, not for each other, but for the common event. (For example, I go to the theater to see a movie, not to interact with the audience.) Because of the episodic nature of collective behavior, people are somewhat more unpredictable than they are in more structured groups. Norms do exist, as we shall see. But they are usually more general and less stringent than in groups that involve direct interaction.

Types of Collective Behavior

Sociologists differentiate among several kinds of collectivities. The following are some examples.

The Crowd.   A crowd is made up of a collection of individuals in physical proximity who exert a mutual influence on each other. Usually they do not know each other (e.g., the spectators at a basketball game). But the reaction of each to the common stimulus has an impact on the others. Excitement is contagious and crowd behavior is exciting. Seventy-five parents watching a little league baseball game are a crowd. They share a common stimulus (the game) and the excitement of the event has impact upon all there. The same group of individuals sitting in a cafeteria after the game are no longer a crowd. There is no common stimulus and no mutual influence.

Crowds may be thought of as three types: the incidental crowd, the organized crowd, and the mob. The first is a casual gathering of individuals who happen to be in the same place at the same time. They wait for a bus on the same street corner or share the same exit from a theater. Their interaction, if indeed they do interact, is limited usually to stereotyped pleasantries. Organized crowds, on the other hand, are spontaneous and share a collective passion that generates great mutual influence. The revivalistic fervor of student pep rallies or the ripe enthusiasm and impassioned activities of some religious congregations illustrate the circular give-and-take of organized crowds. Finally, mobs are the ultimate example of emotional contagion in which suggestability is heightened and may result in destruction and brutality. Lynch mobs and urban riots reveal the vindictive and goal-oriented power of mob action. Individuals are literally caught up in the passionate objective of destroying the hated target. There is a sense of blended identity in which each person loses his or her own responsibility and surrenders to the impetuosity of the group.

Panic Response.   One most interesting area of study in the phenomena of collective behavior is the response of groups of people to threatening situations. Communities that have been confronted with natural disasters or audiences fleeing a fire may be studied to determine panic reaction. Thinkers such as Neil Smelzer point out that panic occurs within certain structural conditions or boundaries.[1] In general, the sequence of panic reaction is as follows:

1. Social conduciveness for panic must be present. Communication must be possible, but "escape routes" must be limited. That is, the everyday social routines and patterns of interaction are confused, but avenues of communication between individuals must be open.

2. In this context, a sudden unanticipated threat appears. This "strain" is defined as an immediate danger. Coupled with the absence of unifying

normative structure, uncomfortable feelings of helplessness are experienced and communicated from one person to another. Uncertainty and ambiguity result and expand into a general apprehension and an atmosphere of irrationality and hysteria.

3. Some precipitating factor occurs that transforms the feeling of vague anxiety into a specific threat. Suspicions are "confirmed" by sensory evidence. Sights, smells, and sounds "prove" the immediacy of the danger.

4. Someone or something becomes a "flight model." This mobilization for flight is a type of leadership and others follow the "leader." This activity heightens the fear and waves of contagious panic increase.

Some research of such panic situations as a storm, war, or floods has suggested that people in crisis situations do not react in wild pandemonium like animals in a stampede.[2] Some people do not panic and refuse to flee. Others are motivated to action by the desire to find and help friends or family or to protect personal possessions. Many citizens begin almost immediately to initiate rescue or recovery actions. Even in disaster, it seems, human beings follow expected and predictable normative rules of behavior acquired by years of social conditioning in nonthreatening contexts.

Public Opinion. The public, as a sociologist would use the words, is a human grouping whose members share a specific position on a given issue. These persons share a common concern about a certain phase of social life. There are, for the sociologist, a number of publics and one individual may be a member of several publics simultaneously.

Public opinion is described as the positions taken by the members of a public regarding a given issue. Public opinion is therefore a type of collective behavior.

Propaganda may be used to sway public opinion. Almost any public issue will be accompanied by the effort to influence public opinion. In such a manner advocates of a specific position hope to gain public support and approval. Advertisers use propaganda effectively to influence public opinion and to sell merchandise. Simple terms and jingles, rather than logic and rational arguments, sell products and get votes. Advertisers use a number of tactics to alter public opinion. Among them are the following:

1. Repetition—Showing and saying the brand name of the product (or politician) facilitates recall and may influence a purchase or a vote.

2. Testimonials—Outstanding and well-known personalities may "endorse" a product.

3. Appeals to popularity—The bandwagon effect, as it is called, points out that everybody else is switching over to such and such candidate.

4. Identification with the common person or average citizen—Antisnobbery is a useful tactic in increasing a potential buyer's sense of belonging. Use of rural areas of scenic beauty or cozy home scenes creates the same feelings of wholesomeness and personal identification with the goods to be bought.

5. Appeals to superiority—Politicians are fond of saying outright that their record or background or abilities are superior to that of their opponent.

Although product advertising does not as often so blatantly compare one item to its competitor, the inference in all advertising is that the product under consideration is the best.

6. Use of stereotypes—An "enemy" may be set up and blamed for some unpleasant situation or evil circumstance. One's opponent, or even a competitive product, is identified directly or by innuendo with the stereotypical enemy. For example, the opponent may "sympathize with the Communists." The reasoning here is that if the public can be persuaded to accept the identification, the negative aspects of the stereotype will be transferred to the opponent.

Rumor.   After the devastating attacks by the Japanese on Pearl Harbor in 1941, thousands of rumors spread through Hawaii and across the United States concerning how the enemy could have facilitated the attack with such precision and success. Many of these stories involved the complicity of local Japanese. These Americans of Japanese ancestry were implicated as saboteurs. They were accused of everything from poisoning the water supply to cutting giant arrows in the cane fields to direct the planes to their targets. Eventually, the United States government acted upon these and other rumors and imprisoned all Japanese-American citizens.

Rumors are one type of communication in collective behavior. When individuals are caught in ambiguous situations, they pool their intellectual resources, so to speak, and invent stories that interpret their ill-defined and confused circumstances. After President Kennedy was assassinated, it was rumored that Lyndon Johnson, then vice president, had suffered a heart attack. Evidently, rumors serve to "explain" and to focus the fear and dread that individuals feel in ambiguous and threatening situations.

Rumors are shaped by the process of communication. True statements and explanations are altered in the telling and become rumors in being passed from one person to another. They change in a number of ways:

1. They may be shortened and made more concise as they are passed from one person to another. This tendency is called *leveling.*

2. They may be *sharpened,* which refers to people's tendency to selectively remember and pass on only a limited number of details.

3. They may be assimilated. *Assimilation* refers to the idea that individuals interpret rumors in the light of their own prejudices and interests. Thus, individuals report what they want to hear when they pass a rumor on.

4. They may be *compounded.* One rumor gives rise to others, and rumors may increase in number with a given incident as people look for interpretation and meaning in confused situations.

Social Movements.   A social movement is an organized activity based upon a response to some unfavorable aspect of society that seeks to achieve some specifically stated objective. Restlessness and spontaneous outbursts against some situation felt to be disagreeable become a social movement when leadership emerges and an organized statement of goals is produced. The feminist movement and civil rights struggle are examples of social movements that have had significant impact on American society in recent years.

The goal of a social movement is reform in which those disagreeable elements of society are rectified. Widespread reform movements may give rise to one or more organizations dedicated to the goal of change. These organizations have an elected (or self-appointed) leadership and a definite membership, and they generate a "we-consciousness."

Movements establish an ideology that consists of norms, values, and attitudes (beliefs) that justify their existence. Slogans, rituals, rallies, songs, and manuals are used to inspire commitment in members and attract new recruits. *Esprit de corps* is necessary to maintain the "we-ness" of the members. An official enemy (i.e., those who help maintain the status quo and thus perpetuate the disagreeable situation) is effectively used to contribute to the "we" feeling by establishing a concrete "they." Tactics for gaining members, holding members, and reaching objectives are developed in an effort to accomplish the movement's goals and reform some segment of society.

Let us turn now to another area of sociological concern. How are individuals and groups in a society systematically ranked and what affect does this ranking have on human behavior?

Stratification

Americans believe in equality. But Americans practice inequality. All people are created equal, we say. And the belief in equality before the law and equality of opportunity is an integral value in our society. At the same time we speak of all being equal, we speak of the haves and have-nots, the disadvantaged, the wrong side of the tracks, the dregs of society, the rich, the social climbers, the power structure, the establishment, and advantages of "good breeding."

Even though we place a premium on equality, we are aware that our society is divided into layers on a scale from high to low and that each layer has a different sized share in socially valued materials and opportunities for the so-called better things in life. The existence of those layers and their content and meaning is what the sociologist calls *stratification.*

Social stratification involves three separate but related factors:

1. It is a socially approved and therefore widespread system of inequality.
2. It is a ranking from superior to inferior of individuals, families, and groups.
3. Each stratum is accorded a prescribed share of social opportunities and socially valued rewards and thus shares a common style of life unique to that layer.

Social stratification may then be defined as a system of social inequality that ranks people and groups into strata according to a specific life-style.

Types of Social Stratification

Methods of ranking individuals into strata vary from one society to another. In general, three systems of stratifying people have emerged in human history: caste, estate, and social class.

Caste. This system, identified with India, is the most clearly graded and rigid type of social stratification. It is characterized by closed categories across which intimate interaction, mobility, and intermarriage are forbidden. One's place in the hierarchy is determined by birth and fixed for life. The strength of the system is that it is justified by the dicta of religion.

India has four castes. (The reader should know that the caste system, while illegal in India, is, like segregation in America, still practiced.)

1. The Priests or Brahmins (6% of the population)
2. The Warriors or Kshatreya
3. The Merchants or Vairya   } 70% of the population
4. The Workers or Peasants or Sudra
5. The Outcastes or Untouchables. These are people who have no caste and they represent 24% of the population.

The whole caste system is based upon an occupational variable in which the caste of the person determines the occupation he will have. Membership is hereditary and marriage is confined within one's caste. Failure to perform according to the rules of caste behavior leads to expulsion from the caste to the level of outcaste and has repercussions not only in this life but in the next several lives the reincarnated individual will have. On the other hand, rigid and faithful adherence to caste rules insures happiness in this life and improvement in the next. Thus, the entire social and economic fiber of India is based upon the caste system.

Estate. This system of stratification is based upon hereditary relationship to the land and its best example is medieval Europe during the time of feudalism. Individuals were placed within one of the following estates in this system of stratification.

The Nobility—The nobles were the political administrators of the system and their military elite. Lord, Baron, Duke, and Count were among the titles used to refer to these individuals. They were the principal aristocracy that controlled and therefore owned the land. The nobility included warriors or men-at-arms, called knights.

The Clergy—Feudal inheritance laws included what is known as primogeniture. That is, the land was inherited by the first-born son. Sons born subsequently became priests. Thus, the upper echelon of the ecclesiastical hierarchy was closely bound to the nobility and enjoyed aristocratic privileges. They were religious counterparts of the nobility.

The Commoners—In exchange for "protection" provided by a lord and his knights, the commoners worked the land and shared the fruit of their labor with the nobility and the clergy. Theirs was subsistence work only in which the aim was to maintain oneself and one's family. No effort was made to make a profit or to improve one's place in life.

Social Class. A social class system differs from both the caste and estate systems in that ranks are open, and individuals are encouraged to move up the social ladder by achievement and progress. Achievement occurs in three areas and thus mobility is based upon self-improvement in each of these areas. The first is the economic sphere. Success in the marketplace is an important variable in American society. One is encouraged to get a good education so as to compete for the better jobs and then to apply oneself in order to be promoted. This variable is referred to by sociologists with the term *class.*

The second area of importance in a social class system of stratification is called *status* and refers to the relative prestige a person is accorded in our society. Prestige is based upon such variables as ancestry, race, education, occupation, and life-style. Thus, status is both ascribed (e.g., ancestry and race) and achieved (e.g., education and occupation). Status is tied to economic variables. The greater the income, the more prestigious the life-style may be. One may live in a better neighborhood, drive more expensive cars, take longer, more exotic vacations, attend (and send children to) better schools, and associate with the more prestigious members of the community. Higher income allows one to consume more conspicuously and therefore to make a claim for more prestige by manipulating more valued status symbols.

Finally, social class is influenced by what sociologists call *power,* which may be defined as the ability to get what you want even over opposition. In our society, power is associated usually with certain social positions. A teacher has power over students, a supervisor over workers, a police officer over motorists, or a chairperson over committee members. The power belongs to the position, not the person. And the person occupying the position may exercise only the legitimate authority accruing to him or her by virtue of the position. For example, teachers do not have absolute power over students.

Class, status, and power, taken together, determine a person's ranking in our society. They are also the avenues through which an individual improves his or her lot through social mobility. People pursue economic and vocational gain. They aspire to prestige and reputation, and they seek control over others and freedom from the control of others.

Slicing the Pie in the United States

Americans, it was said earlier, believe in equality but practice inequality. Equality, it seems, does not mean that rewards are equal. For some interpreters of American stratification, this means that although opportunity is equal, because people differ in incentive, talent, and desire to work, there are differences in size in the slices of the American pie. People, it seems, may be created equal, but some work harder and so they don't stay equal.

Others answer that people have never been equal, not even at birth. Differences in opportunity accrue due to the accident of birth. Black families have consistently earned less income than white families in America. And, according to most research, the gap between the two is closing slowly, if at all.[3] As late as 1975, nonwhite income was only 61 percent of white income, the level of proportion at which it stood in 1970.[4] On the other hand, from 1956-1968, taxlessness among those who made a million dollars a year or more *increased* five-fold, and for those with a $200,000 annual income, the increase was seven-fold![5]

Regardless of the source of the inequality, not everyone gets an equal slice of the pie. Socially valued rewards are distributed unequally. If, for example, we divide the population of this country into fifths, the picture of income distribution would include the following:

1. The top fifth receives approximately 45 percent of the total national income.
   The second fifth receives about 25 percent of the total.
   The third and fourth fifths get about 28 percent.
   The remaining 3 or 4 percent of the national income goes to the botton fifth.
2. This distribution of national income has remained fairly consistent throughout the twentieth century.
3. The major shift in the distribution of income in the last seventy years has occurred in the second and third income fifths. These people, the middle classes, have increased steadily in their share of income. The proportion of the income has increased only slightly for the fourth segment of the income distribution.
4. The bottom fifth, according to some thinkers, has decreased slightly over the last seventy years. But of even more significance, since World War II, while the rest of the country has experienced nearly phenomenal growth in affluence and consumption patterns, the bottom fifth's share in the national income has done no more than remain fairly constant, if indeed it has not fallen.

Inequality in American society also affects what Max Weber, a German sociologist, called one's "life chances." This term means opportunity and includes everything from the chance to live beyond the first year of life, to the chance to acquire an education or eat fine foods or travel or read or live in a comfortable home or avoid being a juvenile delinquent or, if sick, to get well. For Weber, the meaning of social class was that a number of people share a common set of life chances. All these elements promote or impede one's access to economic well-being, status, and power.

The Middle-Class Syndrome

Not all that glitters is gold. The obvious advantages that the middle class possesses in American society may, in the thinking of some, in the long run lead to personality disorders. A way of thinking is necessary for this stratum in our country that may not be mentally healthy.

C. Wright Mills, for example, points out that the basis for middle-class life in America has changed radically.[6] In the nineteenth and early twentieth centuries, the middle class were landowners and shop owners. Well-to-do farmers and small businessmen were the middle class of that day. The new middle class consists of white-collar, salaried employees. Their status is no longer attached to ownership. Education, occupation, authority, and economic achievement are today the important bases of the middle class.

What results may be called an "employee society." Personality is a marketable commodity, and individuals tend to view others in the marketplace as instruments to achieve personal ambition. At the same time employees become "other directed." That is, their motto seems to be "tell me what you desire me to be and I will obey." Since one is dependent upon superiors for promotion (and occupational advancement is necessary), one "sells" one's personality and loyalty, not just skills, to achieve. Salaried, white-collar workers become in Mills' words, "cheerful robots," staying in neutral and going where they are pushed.

Over time, the impersonality and pseudo-friendship of the marketplace comes "home." Relationships with one's family and friends degenerate to the utilitarian level. If, for example, one gives compliments insincerely to gain advantage, how does one know when others are complimenting him or her sincerely?

Robert Presthus sees three personalities emerging in the work world as a result of this middle-class syndrome.[7] First, there are the Upwardly Mobile who react positively to the bureaucracy and succeed in it. They want the rewards of faithfulness, obey the rules to gain advantage, and "make it" in the system. The Indifferents, on the other hand, are uncommitted to the principle of the marketplace and view their jobs as a means to obtain monetary demands of off-work satisfaction. Finally, the Ambivalents are that minority who wish to be upwardly mobile but lack the discipline, or luck, necessary to cash in on the spoils.

To combat the deleterious impact of an impersonal world many call unaffectionately "the rat race," the American middle class has turned in increasing numbers to self-awareness and consciousness-raising programs. Transcendental meditation, sensitivity groups, E.S.T., and assertiveness training offer hope to many in this regard. Americans buy and read books that purport to teach relaxation skills or increase one's capacity to interact adroitly in pressure situations. Popular magazines offer "how to" articles on coping with stress and anxiety. And counselors, psychologists, and psychiatrists arrive early and stay late to accommodate the growing numbers of nervous and restless people looking for help.

Sometimes entire ethnic groups experience the lower rungs of the social ladder. Let's turn our attention to this social phenomenon.

Minorities

The United States has been likened to a melting pot. Beginning in colonial times, people from across the face of the earth left their homelands and put roots down in the New World. The United States, probably more than any other country, has experienced the mingling of people of diverse cultural backgrounds and biological characteristics. It has been what many have called the great experiment in assimilation.

In most instances the members of these varying nationalities have been assimilated into the mainstream of American society. They were enculturated and they lost the unique character of their homeland. They became Americans in the fullest sense of the word. They and their children intermarried with descendants of members of other nationalities and whatever biological uniqueness they might have had was lost.

In other cases, some nationalities have maintained some of the native cultural traits and biological distinctiveness. They and their descendants are Americans, too. But they sometimes preface the word *American* with some notation of their port of origin. They are Mexican-American or Spanish-American or Afro-American or

Japanese-Americans. They are what sociologists, and they themselves, call minorities.

What Is a Minority?

All humans are members of the same species. They are *Homo sapiens*. There are, of course, biological and cultural differences among various groups of homo sapiens. Color is a most obvious biological difference and language quickly comes to mind as a cultural difference. But all people belong to the human race. The concept of a number of human races and of racial differences, it seems, is a social quality. People *believe* that there are different races and that there are social differences among human beings. As a result, people are "grouped" into varieties according to cultural traits and biological characteristics. Because of national and/or cultural boundaries, genetic pools develop that tend to keep certain traits, like skin color or slant of eyes, within a certain population. These boundaries insure the maintenance of the biological and cultural traits within that population.

As stated earlier, people believe that races are different. When people of various "races" live together in the same society, the belief in "social differences" causes some groups to be singled out and subjected to differential treatment. They are identified as a race because they practice a different religion, speak a different language, have a different skin color or hair texture, or because their ancestors came originally from a different country. Sociologists refer to these "social races" as minorities.

Thus, minorities are groups within a society that are distinguished by some observable physical appearance, cultural trait, language, or a combination thereof. They are set apart by the dominant segment of society and receive or are denied certain types of social deference and privilege.

Patterns of Minority Relations

Minorities receive differential treatment. Some minorities, the elite, receive a disproportionate amount of prestige and privilege. They are accorded great wealth and much honor. Not all minorities are so fortunate. Differential treatment for them means less than the average in almost all socially valued rewards.

Some minorities have been *assimilated* through intermarriage and cultural borrowing. The second and third generations of many immigrants to this country have become Americanized through interaction within schools, peer groups, and churches.

Other minorities have been subjected to *segregation*. The legal structure, as well as built-in patterns of discrimination in education, justice, occupation, and housing, have kept them in an inferior position in society.

Stratification is a pattern of minority relations. When segregation is illegal and "separate is recognized as never equal," societies sometimes use ranked strata as a method of keeping minorities "in their place." Here, as in a segregated society, built-in patterns of discrimination insure that the inferior rank of the minority is permanent. The vicious cycle of poverty and poor education and poor jobs and poor housing becomes a way of life for the minority.

Minority business owners can receive help in starting a new business or developing an established one.

Sometimes a minority is simply *annihilated* or *expelled* from a country. Some of the early arrivals to American shores were religious patriots who were expelled as religious minorities from their native land. It was not long until they and other foreigners were busy rendering the same treatment to the American Indian. Where the Indians were not destroyed, they were relegated to a reservation.

Perhaps the most worthy goal in minority relations is *pluralism*. In a pluralistic society, members of various groups keep their cultural and/or biological traits; that is, they keep their "racial identity" but live together in the absence of conflict.

Minority Response to the Dominant Society

Most minorities, as stated earlier, receive a disproportionately small part of socially valued rewards. They are subjected to both prejudice and discrimination. Prejudice is a prejudgment. It is opinion based upon inaccurate and unsupported evidence. Prejudice is both emotional and cognitive; that is, it is a set of attitudes and a set of beliefs. Minorities are judged as inferior to all members of the superior group and, therefore, unworthy of equal rights and privileges. Discrimination, on the other hand, involves behavior toward the minority. Judged as inferior, according to prejudicial attitudes and beliefs, minorities are systematically blocked from economic, political, and social privileges. How do members of minorities respond to these patterns of prejudice and discrimination?

Some minorities are *submissive*. They withdraw into their own communities and live within the socially prescribed boundaries. Or, they may interact among members of the dominant segment of their society according to the accepted rules in order to ingratiate themselves to the more dominant. Dogged loyalty, flattery, and rule-oriented behavior bring their rewards to the individual capable of being an "Uncle Tom."

Other minorities adapt tactics of *resistance*. They may work hard through accepted methods of social mobility, such as education, sports, or business, to become middle-class citizens and enjoy their part in the American Dream.

Another tactic of resistance is riot and violence. Recent American history has contained a chapter concerned with urban frustration among blacks and the resultant bloody city strife. Led by blacks, the explosion against white-dominated society called attention to the intolerable economic and social position of urban minorities.

A final tactic of resistance has been the passive resistance associated with Dr. Martin Luther King, Jr., and his followers. According to the tenets of nonviolent resistance, unjust laws are broken deliberately and the lawbreaker suffers the unjust punishment associated with the law. The intent is that the notoriety that results from such inhuman injustice will appeal to the American conscience and laws will be changed. Using courts and personal betterment, members of minorities, it is reasoned, will be allowed to take their rightful place in American society.

What hope exists for total eradication of prejudice and discrimination in our society is, of course, a question open to debate. Racism is learned. One generation passes it on to the next. How one breaks into that cycle is difficult to answer. But, more importantly, racism becomes institutionalized. The structures of society regarding political and economic power are rigid, and individuals act out discriminatory behavior on the basis of these structures. Ignorance and poverty get built into segments of society as a vicious and unending cycle. Each new generation is subjected to patterns of home life, education, housing, and occupational aspirations and opportunities that the previous generation had. Upon entering the first grade, this new generation is already at a disadvantage due to low educational and occupational achievement of the previous generation. The further these people go on in school, the greater their handicap. When they grow to adulthood and begin families, the cycle starts over again. The disadvantages they suffered by the accident of birth are passed on to their children. In a society in which rewards are passed out in general on the basis of educational, occupational, and political achievement, the children of the dispossessed seem doomed to perpetuate the handicaps of their parents. Breaking up this hopeless cycle of institutionalized racism is by no means an easy task.

But laws have been changed. Affirmative action programs have been instituted. Federal regulations set forth hiring guidelines that insure that race, sex, creed, or color may not be used for or against occupational advancement. Minority organizations have been established to offer assistance and encouragement to individuals seeking to better themselves. Much, of course, remains to be done, but some signs are positive in regard to the creation of a situation in which rewards are more equally shared among the various groups who make up society.

Now let's look at what appears to be an ever-increasing part of human life as we know it. Social scientists of all kinds have long held a fascination with this bit of human behavior.

Human Aggression

People fight. That seems to be a fact of life. In the most harmonious and peace-loving homes, anger can and does erupt. Cities explode with violence and nations go to war. The most industrially capable and scientifically oriented nations make chemical and nuclear weapons while primitive tribes chip spearheads and carve lances.

Sometimes a nation's leadership conspires to destroy an entire race of people from the face of the earth. The evening news becomes a chronicle of today's violence and prime-time TV presents "whodunits" with lifelike battles between the good guys and the bad guys. Aggressiveness is a constant part of human life. Is it instinctual? Or, is it learned? What factors in today's society seem to kindle aggressiveness? Can it be controlled, or at best channeled into nondestructive activity? Or, can we perhaps create a world in which there is no destructive aggression? These questions are of interest to sociologists as they study human behavior. They are also pertinent questions that involve the survival of human kind on this planet.

What Is Aggression?

Football is a violent game in which pain and injury is a way of life. The "good" player is one who seeks to "hit" hard enough to hurt the other in order to gain an advantage for the team. When a player tries to hurt another in order to help win the game, is he being aggressive or is his act simply good competitive sport? How is aggression, as a negative human quality, to be differentiated from more conventional competition?

These questions are usually answered by taking note of two very complicated factors. They are *motive* and *outcome*. Aggression is behavior that is intended to result in injury or harm to another. When an individual intends to hurt another (even if he or she is not successful and no harm results), that person may be said to be engaged in aggressive behavior. The intent (motive) to harm (outcome) is an end in itself and not a means to an end.

What is an aggressive act for one person may not be such for another. Individuals with sanctioned authority, like the police, may intend harm to a person who is involved in an apparent criminal act. They may inflict pain or even take a life, within the boundaries of their authority, to apprehend a suspect. But their aggressiveness is *instrumental;* that is, their act is a means to a socially accepted end and thus socially justified. "Aggressive" football or "aggressive" selling techniques are often justified in the same manner.

Aggression is sometimes openly brutal. Sometimes it is more subtle. Where does, for example, the sanctioned authority of the police end? This is a frequently asked question and by no means easy to answer. Also, is a person showing aggression when he or she votes for a law that has insidious consequences? Is it aggression when one supports or participates in structures of society that affect in a harmful manner large segments of the population? Our question here is concerned with *covert* aggression. That is, is one being aggressive by positively accepting harmful and debilitating aspects of society?

Instinct or Learning

Is humankind aggressive by nature? Some scientists think so. Sigmund Freud, as an example, felt that a human inherits an aggressive instinct that must be funneled into socially acceptable channels. Others, such as Konrad Lorenz, have followed his lead and offer impressive evidence to support their view. Aggressiveness, researchers have pointed out, has helped the species to survive in its "fight" against the obstacles of nature. Archaeologists point out the existence of weapons in the dimmest past of human prehistory. Early cities were walled for defense against attack, and the proclivity for violence and warfare is a recorded fact in human history as far back as it can be traced.

Other scientists, such as Ashley Montagu and Leonard Berkowitz, cite equally impressive evidence that aggressiveness is learned, not instinctual.[8] Prehistoric weapons may have been for hunting and early walls around cities may have been for protection from animals other than humans. Wars began, they feel, only after humans developed civilization and began to collect material wealth as status symbols. A warrior class developed in order to protect the valuables of these city dwellers from invading warriors of other cities.

Thus, the debate goes on. As of now, no final scientific evidence may be offered to settle the question. Which side of the issue one selects depends upon which position one *wants* to believe.

There is, however, one aspect of the issue that few would deny. Human beings may (or may not) be aggressive by nature, but aggression is modifiable by learning. It is known, for example, that aggressive behavior may be created by stimulating a specific section of a monkey's brain. Angry gestures result and the monkey becomes aggressive. But if the monkey is in the presence of a social superior, he runs away. If, on the other hand, that section of the brain is stimulated while the monkey is in the presence of a social inferior, he attacks the other in a hurtful and abusive manner. Thus, it seems that in monkeys learned responses modify aggression.

Aggression and Frustration

The source of aggression, or the trigger that releases aggressive behavior, has been linked by research to frustration. When an individual is thwarted in achieving a goal he or she expects to accomplish, the probability of aggressive reaction is heightened. Pain, boredom, and deprivation are aversive situations that lead to aggression. Children who are told that they may play with a set of attractive toys but who are subjected to a painfully long wait before being allowed to do so become frustrated. It has been found that they smash the toys, throw them about carelessly, and step on them. Other children, not subjected to the long wait, play less destructively and more "normally" with the toys.

It is important to note that expectations must be present before frustrations develop. Children who have no toys do not become angry. They must be both aware of the toys and have some reason to believe they may rightfully play with them before they become frustrated. Adults must be convinced that they have a right to be promoted before becoming frustrated when a company passes them over for another person. What is referred to here is called *relative deprivation*. It is one's deprivation in comparison to what one expects or to what one believes others are receiving. In such a situation, one experiences a crisis of rising expectations, and frustration results and sometimes leads to aggression.

One highly satisfactory explanation of the urban riots of the 1960s and early '70s is found in this crisis of rising expectations. Blacks had been led to expect an improvement in their life situation by the new civil rights laws. They had witnessed the steady growth in affluence of the white middle class since World War II. Television provided them with models of white families living in what seemed to them pure opulence. Expectations rose, but employment and actual life chances did not. Frustration and a sense of hopelessness resulted as they experienced this state of relative deprivation. The outcome is well known. Sections of many American cities became battlegrounds of violence that ended with burned and looted buildings and blood flowing, for the most part, from the veins of black people. An even more recent example of relative deprivation was the frustration associated with the summer gas shortage of 1979. The American expectation of ample gas availability to support a growing appetite for mobility was badly shocked by long lines at the gas station and "out of gas" signs on the gas pumps. Fifty years of the automobile have habituated Americans to a life-style based on cheap and readily available energy sources. Deep resentment and consumer frustration resulted when these expectations were blocked.

It should also be noted that frustration does not always lead to aggressive behavior. Individuals learn a number of methods (some more socially accepted) for handling frustration. The emotional arousal stemming from aversive situations may result in depression, dependency, withdrawal, psychosomatic illness, use of drugs, creative problem solving, or the establishment of alternative goals. How an individual handles frustration depends upon learned responses to this arousal state. Humans, like the electrically stimulated monkey, learn to "run away" in some situations.

TV and Human Aggression

At present rates of television watching, today's average child will have spent 15,000 hours before the TV by the time she or he graduates from high school. He or she will have been exposed to 350,000 commercials and watched 18,000 murders.[9] What is the potential effect of the small screen upon the attitudes and values of today's children? More specifically, what impact will vicarious participation in violence have upon their aggressiveness?

According to the Surgeon General's Scientific Advisory Committee on Television and Social Behavior, the potential impact of TV is both widespread and serious. This committee was established in 1969, spent two full years in study, and produced twenty-three independent research projects and sixty reports and papers. The result of its research was published in a five-volume work. Some of its general findings in general are listed below:

1. Ninety-six percent of American homes have at least one television set.
2. Each set is on for an average of six hours per day.
3. Thirty percent of the dramatic programs are saturated with violence.
4. Seventy percent of all dramatic programs have at least one violent scene.
5. The rate of violent episodes in prime time is eight per hour.
6. Children's cartoons are the single most violent type of program.
7. Violence on TV sells products and is included as a method of maximizing profits.
8. Studies designed to show a causal relationship between TV violence and aggressiveness resulted in elusive and dubious findings.

The meaning of this last mentioned factor is that conclusive proof that viewing violence on TV causes aggressive behavior was not found. This finding has been contradicted by other experimental studies. For example, in February 1977 *Newsweek* quoted Dr. Michael Rathenberg, a child psychiatrist at the University of Washington who has researched twenty-five years of hard data on video violence. His research has included the fifty most comprehensive studies involving over 10,000 children from diverse backgrounds. According to this *Newsweek* article, Dr. Rathenberg found that most of these studies conclude that viewing violence on TV tends to produce aggressiveness in children.[10] Again, according to the article, early in February 1977 the American Medical Association declared that television violence is a mental-health problem. This normally conservative association called upon ten major corporations (such as General Motors and Sears, Roebuck) to review their advertising policies for sponsoring violent shows.

It is known that children do imitate aggressive behavior after seeing it demonstrated. Albert Bandura and his associates have shown the extent of aggressive imitation in their classic set of experiments with plastic, airfilled BoBo dolls.[11] These dolls are bottom heavy and when knocked down will return to an upright position. Some children observed adults hitting the dolls. Others saw adults hit the dolls and abuse them verbally. Still others watched as adults hit the dolls, abused them verbally, and were then rewarded with praise for their activity. All three groups of children, when allowed to play with the dolls, imitated the adult behavior. The most enthusiastically aggressive group of children were the group who had observed aggressive behavior being rewarded.

Again, according to the *Newsweek* article cited earlier, ABC commissioned a study of 100 juvenile offenders and found that no fewer than twenty-two confessed to having imitated criminal techniques from watching TV. Other research has concluded that individuals predisposed to violent reactions have that propensity heightened by TV violence. Others note that TV violence increases the tolerance for violence and creates an indifference toward human suffering.[12]

Experimental evidence on the relationship of TV violence and human aggression is, therefore, inconclusive. Television producers, who note that parents should be responsible for what children watch, continue to spin off the nightly carnage of violent entertainment.

Perhaps researchers as well as concerned parents and others have been asking the wrong question. We have asked, "Does viewing violence on TV do anyone harm?" Maybe the question should be, "What good does video violence do?" What positive effects does watching raw aggression have on children, or, for that matter, on adults?

The impact of television on economic, social, and political life is, as yet, unknown. The long-range effect of TV on American life-style will no doubt be significant. It seems nothing less than foolhardy to allow so pervasive an influence to affect social values and behavior without at the very best knowing what changes are occurring.

Summary

Among the many areas of concern that sociologists look into are collective behavior, stratification, race relations, and aggression. This chapter has focused upon those specific subjects because they are representative of sociological inquiry and because the probability is great that most readers of this text are involved in some way in each of these areas.

Collective behavior is gatherings of individuals in which a common stimulus is occurring and interaction and mutual influence are at a minimum. These events are episodic and are, therefore, less structured than more formal groups.

Stratification refers to socially approved rankings of individuals and groups from inferior to superior based upon a common share in socially valued materials. Caste, estate, and social class systems of stratification are methods of such rankings. In the United States, stratification occurs within the social class system. That is, individuals are ranked by virtue of their *class* (economic well-being), *status* (prestige level), and *power* (control over their own lives). Despite the common belief in equality that characterizes the American society, much inequality exists.

The study of relationships between the dominant segment of society and subordinate ethnic groups is called race or minority relations. Believing races to be real and believing racial differences to exist, members of society follow norms that relegate sections of society to inferior positions. Set apart by biological and/or cultural differences, these minorities are considered "races." A number of patterns of race relations have developed in history among which are assimilation, segregation, stratification, expulsion, and pluralism.

Aggression is the deliberate attempt to do another harm or injury. Some scholars say it is instinctual and thus a natural part of human life and personality. Others disagree and posit the learned nature of aggression. All agree, however, that aggression may be modified by learning. Aggression stems from frustrated goals, although not all frustration leads to aggression.

Notes

1. Neil Smelzer, *Theory of Collective Behavior* (New York: The Free Press, 1963).

2. Enrico W. Quarantelli, "Images of Withdrawal Behavior in Disasters: Some Basic Misconceptions," *Social Problems 8* (Summer 1960): 68-79.

3. See Howard M. Bahr et al., *American Ethnicity* (Lexington, Mass.: D.C. Heath and Co., 1979), p. 168.

4. Ibid., p. 169.

5. Phillip Stern, "How 381 Super Rich Americans Managed Not to Pay a Cent in Taxes Last Year," *The New York Times Magazine,* 13 April 1969, p. 114.

6. C. Wright Mills, *White Collar* (New York: Oxford University Press, 1951).

7. Robert Presthus, *The Organizational Society,* rev. ed. (New York: St. Martin's Press, 1978), pp. 100ff.

8. For an excellent summary of these two points of view, see Leonard Berkowitz, "The Case for Bottling Up Rage," *Psychology Today* 7 (July 1973): 24-31.

9. "What T.V. Does to Kids," *Newsweek,* 21 February 1977, pp. 63ff.

10. Ibid., p. 63.

11. Albert Bandura, "Vicarious Processes: No-Trial Learning," in *Advances in Experimental Psychology,* ed. Leonard Berkowitz (New York: Academic Press, 1968), pp. 15ff.

12. "What T.V. Does to Kids," *Newsweek,* p. 67.

Additional Readings

Aronson, Elliot. *The Social Animal.* San Francisco: W. H. Freeman and Co., 1972.

Bahr, Howard M. et al. *American Ethnicity.* Lexington, Mass.: D.C. Heath and Co., 1979.

Bandura, Albert. "Vicarious Processes: No-Trial Learning." In *Advances in Experimental Psychology,* edited by Leonard Berkowitz. New York: Academic Press, 1968.

Blumer, Herbert. "Social Movements." In *New Outline of Principles of Sociology,* edited by A. M. Lu. New York: Barnes and Noble, 1951.

Conot, Robert. *Rivers of Blood, Years of Darkness.* New York: Bantam Books, 1967.

Harrington, Michael. *The Other America: Poverty in the United States.* Baltimore: Penguin Books, 1962.

Hodges, Harold M., Jr. *Social Stratification: Class in America.* Cambridge, Mass.: Schenkman, 1964.

Lorenz, Konrad. *On Aggression.* New York: Harcourt Brace Jovanovich, 1966.

Masotti, Louis et al. *A Time to Burn.* Chicago: Rand McNally, 1969.

Montagu, Ashley, ed. *Man and Aggression,* 2d ed. London: Oxford University Press, 1973.

Presthus, Robert. *The Organizational Society,* rev. ed. New York: St. Martin's Press, 1978.

Schneider, David J. *Social Psychology.* Reading, Mass.: Addison-Wesley Publishing Co., 1976.

Smelser, Neil J. *Theory of Collective Behavior.* New York: The Free Press, 1963.

four

Sociology and the City

Humankind has been on earth for approximately 3½-5 million years. Modern humans (i.e., humans with the physiques and mental capacities of today's individuals) appeared approximately 60,000 years ago. During most of those thousands of years, humans existed without cities, living as wandering bands of hunters and gatherers. Primitive, permanent communities appeared about 8000 B.C., and cities were invented about 5,000 years ago. As recently as 200 years ago, the world's population was predominately rural. Since then, cities have come to dominate the earth and urbanism has become a way of life. As the characteristic life-style of human beings, cities are an extremely recent social invention, and the sudden emergence of cities to their present place of prominence may rightly be termed an explosion.

As recently as 1800, less than 8 percent of the world's population lived in cities with more than 5,000 residents. By the year 2000, it is projected that a majority of the earth's inhabitants will live in urban places.

Even in underdeveloped nations, urban growth has been phenomenal. According to the *United Nations Demographic Yearbook, 1972,* of the ten largest cities in the world, five were in Asia, two were in Europe, and one was in North America (see Table 1).

In the United States, the urban explosion has occurred more rapidly than in most other parts of the world. In 1790, the year of the first census, approximately 5 percent of the American population of 4 million was urban. In 1970, that figure was 74

Table 1. *World's Most Populous Cities, 1970*

City	Size
1. Shanghai	10,820,000
2. Tokyo	8,841,000
3. New York	7,895,000
4. Peking	7,570,000
5. London	7,379,000
6. Moscow	7,050,000
7. Bombay	5,969,000
8. Seoul	5,536,000
9. Sao Paulo	5,187,000
10. Cairo	4,961,000

percent. Of the 27 percent living in rural areas, less than 6 percent were engaged in agriculture. Again, in 1790, there were only 24 cities of more than 2,500 population. Philadelphia was the largest city with a population of 42,000; New York followed with 33,000; Boston, Baltimore, and Charleston came next with 10,000 to 25,000. The other 19 cities had populations of less than 10,000. In contrast, today there are almost 5,000 cities of more than 2,500 population and 247 of those are what the Census Bureau calls Standard Metropolitan Statistical Areas (SMSA) (cities and surrounding area of more than 50,000 population).

The dramatic shift from rural to urban places of residence may be illustrated by the percentage of the labor force engaged in agriculture. In 1800, 75 percent of the adult males in U.S. society were farmers. By 1880, that figure was reduced to 50 percent. In 1940, the percentage was about 20 percent, and today it is less than 5 percent.

The urban explosion in our country occurred while the population was growing rapidly both by natural increase and by immigration. (From 1900 to 1914, almost a million people immigrated each year and almost all these immigrants took up residence in cities.) Americans forsook the farms and moved to town. By 1920, more than half of the population was urban. And not only did they move to town, they showed an appetite for the larger cities. It is projected that by the year 2000, better than half of the U.S. population will reside in two urban regions or giant cities. Forty-one percent will live in the Chicago to New York to Washington "city" and 14 percent will live in the southern California "city."

Urbanization and Urbanism

A distinction must be made between the two terms, *urbanization* and *urbanism*. The former refers to the geographic movement of people from the rural to the urban area. The statistics in the preceding section reflect urbanization in various parts of the world and specifically in America. Urbanization, then, is a demographic process and refers to the relative proportion of a population living in an urban place. Urbanism, on the other hand, connotes a condition or quality of life that is associated with urban living. It is used in reference to behavioral factors of city living.

Some areas of the world have experienced urbanization but little urbanism. Cairo, as an example, is the world's tenth largest city. Yet the people who live there remain largely rural in life-style and orientation. Also, while the census records about 27 percent of the U.S. population as rural, the agents of socialization, especially the school and the mass media, have virtually urbanized the entire nation. Some thinkers, such as Maurice Stein in his *Eclipse of Community*,[1] note that the concepts rural and urban, as descriptive of unique life-styles, are no longer useful in studying American society. The cultural patterns of the populace of American society, regardless of place of residence, is almost totally dominated by urban attitudes and life-styles.

The Characteristics of the City

All cities share certain common features. No city, for example, is self-supporting. A city depends upon the rural area for provisions of food and fiber. In U.S. society, the products that city folk buy come from farmers across the nation and, in some cases, from all over the world. Rural areas provide the raw materials that are formed into the goods that the urbanite (and the ruralite) consume. Thus, the city is dependent upon farmers with enough surplus to feed the city dwellers.

Cities are also dependent upon other cities for products and trained people not available in the immediate area. So specialized has our world become that cities become identified with a specific function that other cities become dependent upon. New York is the communications center, Washington the center of the federal government, Detroit the automobile center, Pittsburgh the steel center, and Miami the resort center of the nation. Smaller cities may also serve a single function for a region or the entire nation. What do you think of when you hear the following names: Las Vegas, Nevada; Vail, Colorado; Princeton, New Jersey; Nashville, Tennessee; Taos, New Mexico; or Green Bay, Wisconsin?

A second common feature of the city is a complex division of labor. Cities offer a wide range of occupational choice and specialization. Indeed, one reason for the phenomenal growth of cities in the last two hundred years is the occupational range offered within its boundaries. A single factory, as an example, is made up of top level executives, junior executives and their various divisions and assistants, workers from superintendents to laborers, secretaries, file clerks, janitors, and maintenance personnel. Modern society is dedicated to the proposition that by concentrating on one small area of concern, people will be more efficient in their tasks. Medical doctors specialize in various parts of the human body. Lawyers specialize in various aspects of the law. Football players specialize in various functions of the sport. Teachers specialize in various aspects of their discipline. Restaurants specialize in various types of food. Laborers specialize in various crafts. The city, by providing a wide-ranging clientele, encourages this specialization.

The city is also characterized by heterogeneity. Inhabitants of the city differ in almost all respects from one another. Urbanites differ in life-styles, physical attributes, religious outlooks, political beliefs, socioeconomic positions, and recreational outlets. They represent a wide range of cultural and social backgrounds and seem to tolerate individual and group peculiarities more readily than do rural dwellers.

The city is usually characterized by a faster pace and, at times, by social disorganization and conflict. The heterogeneity of the city and its emphasis upon specialization tends to encourage the development of interest groups who, at times, may be at variance with one another. Thus, no city exists that does not make provision for such organizations as the police that help to control the population. Elected officials, the mass media, and other organizations, such as labor unions and concerned citizen groups, may also help to direct and control unrest and disorganization.

Finally, cities are internally interdependent. The units of social organization that make up a city are functionally significant and each unit depends upon all others to a greater or lesser degree. When one unit fails to operate (or refuses to do so as in a strike), the entire city feels the consequences. Sanitation workers, it seems, are as important in a functional sense as are politicians, teachers, and medical doctors.

The City as a Way of Life

Since 1915, with the beginnings of the study of human ecology at the University of Chicago, American sociologists have researched the city as a way of life. Robert E. Park, Ernest Burgess, and R.D. McKenzie and their students were interested in how people interact in the city and what effect city life has on its inhabitants.[2] In general, these early pioneers of urban sociology looked at various social problems, such as juvenile delinquency, gang behavior, suicide, and prostitution, and plotted the distribution of their occurrence across a city map. They discovered that these behaviors occurred more frequently in the deteriorating area surrounding the central business district, which they called the *zone of transitions*.

In 1938, Louis Wirth, a student of Park and Burgess, published an article entitled "Urbanism as a Way of Life."[3] His intent was to specify the characteristics of interaction in the urban world. His conclusions may be summarized as follows:

1. The city is impersonal and rational in orientation. People are utilitarian in outlook and tend to view others as a means to an end. The result is a very dehumanized set of relationships.

2. The city tolerates and rewards differences in its inhabitants. Unique life-styles abound.

3. Social control is weakened and left to formal agencies. Public opinion and individual ostracism are ineffective because of heightened anonymity among city dwellers.

4. Communication is by mass media and the individual finds expression of himself or herself only through groups of which he or she is a part.

Others, like Harold L. Wilensky and Charles N. Lebeaux in *Industrial Society and Social Welfare*,[4] argue that, while Wirth was correct in his analysis of Chicago in the early 1900s, what he described was a passing phenomenon. Chicago, they note, during the era Wirth described, had been subjected to wave after wave of foreign immigrants. Rapid urbanization, especially from the rural South to the Northern urban centers, had brought an influx of newcomers to the city. What Wirth described was not the quality of city life but the quality of life in a city that had recently undergone sudden and extensive growth. The resultant social disorganization, disorientation, and dehumanization was a function not so much of the city as of urban expansion. Further, Wilensky and LeBeaux note that the industrial order, with its rising affluent society, had created a much less impersonal city. As evidence, they pointed to the suburbs with their friendship groups, their strong family ties and home orientation, and their passive contentment with campers, boats, and barbecue pits.

Herbert Gans offers another interesting point of view on the urban life-style. In his article "Urbanism and Suburbanism as Ways of Life," [5] he insists that the "urbanite" is a product of mass society and not the creature of the city per se. The city, as distinguished from the suburbs, is made up of a number of subcultures. Gans lists five:

1. The *cosmopolites*. These people remain in the city because they wish to receive the unique cultural benefits of the urban area. They are intellectuals and professional and are usually artistically inclined.

2. The *unmarried or childless*. Residence in the city is reflective of the stage of the life cycle in which these people presently are. They live in apartment areas and enjoy the night action of single life. When they marry or, with the arrival of their first child, they ordinarily move to the suburbs.

3. *Ethnic villagers*. This group of city dwellers sometimes occupy as much as a total single census tract and make up a rather stable community.

4. The *deprived*. These people, making up poor and usually unstable families, remain in the city because there is nowhere else to go. They reside in slumlike conditions and make up what is known as the urban ghetto.

5. The *trapped and downwardly mobile*. This last group, which overlaps the fourth groups, can't compete in society any longer. They are debilitated by age or other infirmities and include derelicts as well as the very young and very old.

Gans seems to be saying that the city is made up of a diverse heterogeneous population that, in many ways, shares a common way of life. The city, he argues, is a conglomeration of dissimilar groups. There is no one "way of life" in the city. The city is a meeting place and working place for people of different interests, skills, and needs and, as such, reflects a number of life-styles.

The city dweller, nonetheless, is characteristically reserved, according to J. John Palen in *The Urban World*.[6] Palen notes that the urbanite is goal-oriented and that rationality and calculation replace the warm human relationships. City life moves at a fast pace. This statement means that modern urbanites are subjected to an overwhelming number of stimuli. To protect themselves from overstimulation, city dwellers respond with anonymity and calculated impersonality. They are blasé. They become brusque; they disregard low priority stimuli; they shift the burden of responsibility to others; they shut people out with unlisted phone numbers and locked apartment gates; they seek privacy behind tall fences and refuse to become involved.

Symbiosis is a significant term, borrowed from biology, that sociologists use to describe the nature of most role relationships within the urban setting. Individuals need other people but not as specific individuals. Rather, they need them as a category. For example, the people who operate the electric power plants for a town are important to the total community. We depend upon them in a very specific way. Yet, it is not the specific individuals which we need. What is needed is simply any trained, capable set of people who know how to keep the lights on in our homes. The relationship that we have with power plant operators is a symbiotic one. Most relationships that we have in the urban setting are of this rather inhumane type. We need other people to do things for us, and they, in turn, need us to do for them.

The City Image

Thomas Jefferson once said that agriculture was God's appointed vocation for humankind. He feared a country of urban domination and wanted to keep the folks "down on the farm." Implied in his ideas is an image or stereotype of the city that many Americans still share. The city is viewed in a rather negative fashion. It, for many Americans, is little better than a necessary evil. One must live there for it is in the city where one finds work. But one must devise means to escape from it. In this stereotype, the rural areas are seen as made up of stable, slow-moving communities. Norms and roles reflect this same stability. Relationships are seen as personal and warm. Tradition is strong, and cultural conformity and social continuity are a part of life. The city, on the other hand, is viewed as complex. Innovation and change make life temporary. Relationships are transient, cold, and detached. City people are private intellectuals and have less warmth and genuine feelings. Rural people are real.

The adoration of the rural tradition and agrarian roots dies slowly. Americans perpetuate it with strong symbols in the culture. Subdivisions are given rural sounding names like Timber Creek, Meadow Park, and Rolling Acres. Billboards advertising these residential areas to crowded highways of commuters hawk the open spaces and freedom these "country estates" have. Children's books are filled with pictures and stories of the rural areas. Everything from "The Three Pigs," "Red Riding Hood," and "Goldilocks and the Three Bears" pays homage to the rural way of life. Advertisers take advantage of this American nostalgia for rural values. Cereals are "natural and filled with old-fashioned" taste. The Marlboro man rides the open range, and handsome young people wade clear wilderness streams smoking Salems. Politicians avoid being identified with the establishment and the sophisticated, urbane intellectual. Rather, they wish to be seen as "just common folk."

On the other hand, cities are viewed as perverse places of slums and crime. Cities create more problems than they can solve. According to the stereotype, they are unwholesome for raising children and have an unhealthy effect on family morals. Politicians, lawyers, and big business are corrupt. City people are highly paid for doing little work. City churches are secularized and have lost contact with "true spirituality." City schools are hot beds for drugs, teenage sex, and crime. City people cannot walk the streets at night. Muggings and rapes occur in open daylight in the presence of witnesses who watch passively and refuse to aid the victim.

There is, of course, some truth in these stereotypes. But, there is also some error. The point is that the myth helps to create the part of the stereotype that is true. The values that undergird the positive attitude toward the countryside and the negative attitudes toward the city help to increase the decay of the city. Too few Americans actually love the cities where they live. They seem to take a utilitarian view of the community, expecting much from it and using it toward that end but contributing little, and then only begrudgingly, to it. Young people return to farming to escape city life. Whites, as soon as they can do so financially, flee further from the city's center to the suburbs. Americans love the wilderness and the great outdoors and seek to preserve it. And we should do so. But, we are an urban society and probably will remain urban. "Save our city" is as worthy a cry as "save our wilderness." Programs geared to humanizing the city and making it a more healthy social environment for people to live in are as necessary in our times as preserving the physical environment.

Cities face staggering problems today. Sheer numbers is the first of these. Increased agricultural technology forced many from the rural sector into the city. Rapid expansion in industry- and service-oriented occupations provided jobs in the cities. Beginning in the 1950s slums resulted from this *in*-migration. Certain areas in large cities afforded newcomers' cheap, though crowded, housing. Patterns of residential segregation made it impossible for many of these inhabitants to move out even when they were financially able to do so. Physical deterioration and population density increased as well as the frustration from being trapped. Unemployment followed. Slum dwellers' educational opportunities declined and further trapped the slum dwellers in the ghetto subculture.

The city—expanding, impersonal, hectic, exciting, complex, dehumanizing,...

Crime increased. Without employment opportunities individuals turned to illegal activities for income. Alcoholism and drug use heightened these trends. The family lost control over children and was increasingly replaced by peer-group influence. Fatherless families increased as husbands were unable to support their families and left in search of better opportunities. Matriarchal arrangements began to dominate.

As the central city declined, whites who could afford to do so moved out. This phenomenon, called *white flight,* mushroomed the suburbs and left the central city filled with low-income families and had the effect of shrinking the tax base of the city. Confronted with increasing demands for social services and police protection, the city found itself with fewer tax dollars for support. They needed new schools, bigger hospitals, street maintenance, and more utilities, which simply could not be provided. The central city deteriorated further.

In the seventies, new problems began to appear in the form of energy shortage. Unusually severe winters made demands on already deficient energy supplies. Schools and businesses closed and many city services had to be curtailed. Americans, always notorious as energy wasters, were confronted with the sudden realization that the resources of the earth were finite and their way of life built upon unparalleled use of raw materials could not continue indefinitely.

The city is a complex social arrangement that humans invented. Its size and the immense problems it creates for human life demand innovation and creativity. Sudden growth has brought about unanticipated negative consequences. Desmond Morris, in his book *The Human Zoo*,[7] likens the city and its modern problems for human existence to a zoo. Animals in the wild are orderly and generally peaceful. When caged, they are placed in a situation for which the long process of evolution has left them unprepared. In zoos, animals engage in all types of aberrant behavior. The natural flow of life is interrupted and they respond with deviance. Humans are not unlike other animals. Our long evolutionary history has failed to prepare us for the city and, like animals in a zoo, we respond in an unnatural manner to our confines. But, we are adaptable. The city is our way of life and we are unlikely to return to the "wild." Thus, the city must be transformed to more human dimensions. Careful planning at the national and local level is necessary as well as changes in laws and values. To succeed is to create a better world. To fail is to make life virtually impossible.

The Suburbs

The Origin of Suburbs

Suburbs as we know them today began with upperclass summer homes in rural areas. The affluent of the city left for extended vacations in these rural enclaves and returned during school months to their jobs and schools in the city. These villages of summer homes were located on railroad lines and only the rich could afford the luxury of suburban living. Their dream was to combine the conveniences of the city with the benefits of rural life. That dream, available to the rich, remains the driving force today behind the movement to the suburbs.

The Suburban Myth

Studies of suburbia as well as popular magazine and newspaper articles have usually focused upon a single suburb or at best one type of suburb. The effort is made to generalize from this biased sample to all suburbs. The result is a stereotype of suburbia based upon a myth. Suburbs come in a number of variations. They may be rich or poor, black or white, old or new, liberal or conservative, attractive or ugly. No one single life-style is characteristic of suburbia.

Perhaps the most useful differentiation between suburbs (but here again generalizations are dangerous) is between white-collar, middle-class suburbs and blue-collar, working-class suburbs. In general, residents of the former are WASP (white, Anglo-Saxon, Protestant), young, well educated, hold white collar occupations, are upwardly mobile and family oriented. In addition, neighboring is important.

Blue-collar suburbs include very little neighborhood interaction or visiting. Inhabitants are wage earners and show little aspirations for social mobility. They exhibit no revival of religiosity and remain conservative in life-style and democratic in political outlook. They are not joiners. In short, blue-collar workers who live in the suburbs do not differ significantly in life-style from their counterparts who remain in the city.

Suburban fertility rates are not appreciably higher than that of the city in general. Suburbs may have a disproportionate number of children, that is true. However, suburbia has had a disproportionate number of couples of child-bearing age. Since one important reason for the move to the suburbs has been that the suburban environment is deemed "better for children," more couples with small children have felt the need for migration to the suburbs. Childless couples and those whose children are grown feel less constraint to move and are more likely to remain in the city.

In some suburbs, people are seldom seen outside their homes.

The Suburban Future

Rising costs of individual transportation as well as rising costs of materials and labor to build new homes may see some curtailment in suburban growth. National commitment to the rejuvenation of the inner city as well as energy shortages may make the free-standing, single family dwelling unit a thing of the past. High-rise apartment buildings and condominiums may replace suburban sprawl. Already the price of a new home, high interest and utility rates, and the expense of commuting have placed the option of owning a new home outside the framework of low-income families. How Americans will react to these realities of urban life remain to be seen.

Let us now turn to a discussion of urban trends in the underdeveloped nations of the world.

Urban Growth in Underdeveloped Nations

The term *underdeveloped* is only one among many used to describe most countries in Latin America, Africa, and Asia. Other terms include *developing nations, modernizing nations,* and *the Third World.* All these terms are polite ways of saying "poor" nations. The Third World includes two-thirds of the world's population but accounts for only one-sixth of the world's income, one-third of the world's food production, and one-tenth of the world's industrial output. It is a world of a few rich and powerful and many poor and powerless. Its people are largely illiterate and agrarian and are forced to live on protein-deficient diets in backward and primitive conditions.

Developing nations, as a rule, have the highest population rates in the world. If one excludes China, the population of the Third World was 1.8 billion in 1970. By the year 2000, it is projected to be 3.6 billion. The underdeveloped nations grow at an annual rate of 2½-3 percent, which means they double in population every 15-20 years. Population growth in these nations may be attributed to the reduction of death rates and the retention of birth rates. Modern medicine, sanitary improvements, and increased (even if inadequate) food supply have lowered the death rates significantly since World War II. Efforts to lower the birth rate have been either nonexistent or ineffective.

Some of these nations are poor (and some even impoverished) because of limited industrialization and economics based largely upon agriculture. Economic and industrial expansion is difficult at best. In the context of growing population with new mouths to feed and increased demand for public services, governments in these nations find it impossible to raise the standard of living. Any improvement in national growth is quickly gobbled by an increasing population so that developing nations are hard pressed to maintain the status quo. Of significance is the impact of technology on improved industrialization in these nations. Nineteenth-century expansion of industry in the United States and in Europe included the demand for unskilled labor. Low pay and low skill jobs provided employment opportunities for ruralites (and immigrants) who moved to town. But improved technology in the third quarter of the twentieth century has created highly mechanized industrial growth in the Third World. As a result, when industry does expand in these nations, little growth takes place in employment opportunities. It is not infrequent to find unemployment rates in these nations exceeding 25 percent.

Urbanization in the Third World

Underdeveloped nations are poor and growing poorer. They are overpopulated and growing more populous. And they are experiencing unprecedented urbanization. Put in a nutshell, Third World peasants are leaving the farm to move to town because there is nowhere else to go. They are pushed from the rural areas because village and countryside poverty is worse than any poverty one may find in the city. No jobs may be found in the rural districts and there is at least the hope of some work in the city. Nineteenth- and early twentieth-century Americans were pulled into the cities by economic and industrial expansion. Jobs awaited them. But Third World citizens of today move to the city with only the faint glimmer of employment. For most, the glimmer fades in disappointment.

The rate of urbanization is alarmingly high in the Third World. Latin America, commonly thought of as rural, is more urban than Europe (54 percent as compared to 53 percent). Egypt has a higher percentage of urban dwellers than either France or Sweden. Cities of 100,000 or more in the Third World are growing at a rate of 67 percent per decade. One-third of the world's urban population is in developing nations. And these nations contain some of the world's largest cities. Indeed, six of the ten largest cities in the world are in the Third World: Shanghai, Peking, Bombay, Seoul, Sao Paulo, and Cairo.

Overurbanization

The term *overurbanization* is sometimes used to describe this phenomenon in the Third World. These nations remain largely rural in values, orientation, and technology. The rate of urbanization exceeds the capacity of the cities to absorb and care for new residents. The need for public services, such as sewers, water, and electricity, as well as the availability of food and jobs in these cities is exceeded by the proportion of the population residing in urban places.

Housing is perhaps the most dramatic example of the shortages created by overurbanization. The cities of the Third World are ringed by what may be called "shanty towns." Located on the most undesirable land area, such as hillsides, garbage dumps, and swamps, the "suburban" housing are literally covered by tarpaper and cardboard "houses" in which recent arrivals to the city live. No sewers or water supply serves these communities. Electricity is the only modern convenience that some residents enjoy.

Large percentages of urban dwellers reside in these squatter cities, and national governments seem to be incapable of doing anything about it. According to Palen in *The Urban World*,[8] shanty towns have grown astronomically in population since the end of World War II. He notes, for example, that in the metropolitan areas of Peru residents in shanty towns increased from 45,000 in 1945 to almost a million in 1960. Of the five million in Lima, Peru, in 1975, a million and a quarter (approximately 25 percent) live in squatter towns. In Caracas, the capital of Venezuela, about 35 percent of the population live in shanty towns.

Because of rapid increases in population, the average age of the citizens of developing nations is much younger than that of Europe and America. How to feed this swelling mass of humanity, much less to clothe and house it, is a question beyond the means of most developing nations. Energy shortages along with severe weather conditions make the food problem of the future most severe in these nations. Questions of life quality and environmental concerns are not even asked. Solutions to these problems must await answers to the more immediate and pressing questions of providing food. Overpopulation and compression of this burgeoning population into cities have stretched the earth's resources and human ingenuity near the breaking point.

Summary

Urbanization (the process of urban migration) and urbanism (the quality of life characteristic of the city) are common facts of life in today's world. Since its invention about 10,000 years ago, humankind has shown an increasing hunger for the amenities of city life. However, it has only been in the last two hundred years that conditions were such that more than a handful of the earth's population could live in cities. Today, those conditions have made it possible for the majority of the world's masses to reside in cities. By the year 2000, that trend will be complete and over half of the world will live in cities.

Cities share certain characteristics in common. Among them are dependency on rural areas, complex division of labor, heterogeneity, faster pace, disorganization, and internal interdependence.

Since early in the twentieth century, sociologists have been interested in the city as a way of life. With few notable exceptions, the quality of life of the city has been described as rational and utilitarian in orientation. City dwellers are seen as characteristically reserved and blasé, and life within the city is viewed as impersonal as city dwellers seek to avoid the overstimulation that is a natural occurrence of their fast paced life. As a result of research and in common with much popular writing on the subject, the city has gained a somewhat negative image that includes high crime rates, cold and detached relationships, pseudo-intellectualism and snobbery, and slums. This stereotype is, in part, true. Cities today confront overwhelming problems of crime, overpopulation, housing, traffic, shrinking taxes, physical deterioration, and increasing demand for social services.

For many, the solution to the cities' problems has been to move to the suburbs. The popularity of suburbs and the suburban myth has persisted in our society. But with potentially severe energy shortages on the horizon and the price of home building escalating rapidly, what the future holds for the ideal of a free-standing, single-family home in the suburbs is anybody's guess.

Urbanization has occurred rapidly in industrialized nations of Europe and North America. It is increasing even more rapidly in the underdeveloped nations of the Third World. One significant reason for this is rapid population growth. A second factor is that rural dwellers are migrating to the city because of undesirable conditions in their home villages. Largely rural in orientation and with unemployment rates as high as 25 percent, the giant urban centers of developing nations offer little respite for the poverty and hopelessness of these newcomers. As a result, most large cities in the Third World are ringed by squatter villages and thousands of jobless, impoverished, and hungry masses. Despite the overurbanization of these nations, their cities are among the largest in the world and are growing more rapidly than cities of the industrialized West. The sheer press of population, and the problems of getting food for this growing mass of humanity, overshadow any other urban concern of the governments of developing nations. Indeed, these problems may already be too overwhelming for these governments to solve.

Notes

1. Maurice Stein, *The Eclipse of Community: An Interpretation of American Community Studies* (Princeton, N.J.: Princeton University Press, 1960), p. 56.
2. For an excellent history and evaluation of the Chicago school of human ecology see Dennis E. Paplin, *Communities: A Survey of Theories and Methods of Research* (New York: The Macmillan Co., 1972), pp. 65-105.
3. Louis Wirth, "Urbanism as a Way of Life," *American Journal of Sociology* 44 (July 1938): 10.
4. Harold L. Wilensky and Charles N. LeBeaux, *Industrial Society and Social Welfare* (New York: The Free Press, 1965), pp. 121-33.
5. Herbert J. Gans, "Urbanism and Suburbanism as Ways of Life: A Reevaluation of Definitions," in *Urban America,* ed. J. John Palen and Karl H. Flaming (New York: Holt, Rinehart and Winston, 1972), pp. 184-200.
6. J. John Palen, *The Urban World* (New York: McGraw-Hill, 1975), pp. 116ff.
7. Desmond Morris, *The Human Zoo* (New York: Dell Publishing Co., 1969), pp. 8-12.
8. Palen, *The Urban World,* pp. 324, 325.

Additional Readings

Berger, Bennet B. "The Myth of Suburbia." *Journal of Social Issues* 17 (1971): 328-47.

Davis, Kingsley. "Burgeoning Cities in Rural Countries." In *Scientific American, Cities: Their Origin, Growth, and Human Impact.* San Francisco: W.H. Freeman and Co., 1973.

_____ . "The Origin and Growth of Urbanization in the World." *American Journal of Sociology* 60 (March 1955): 291-99.

Gans, Herbert J. *The Urban Villagers,* Glencoe, Ill.: Free Press, 1962.

_____ . "Urbanism and Suburbanism as Ways of Life: A Reevaluation of Definitions." In *Urban America,* edited by J. John Palen and Karl H. Flaming. New York: Holt, Rinehart and Winston, 1972.

Hartley, Shirley Foster. *Population Quantity vs. Quality.* Englewood Cliffs, N.J.: Prentice-Hall, 1972.

Hawley, Amos. *Urban Society.* New York: Ronald Press, 1971.

Palen, J.John. *The Urban World.* New York: McGraw-Hill, 1975.

Thomlinson, Ralph. *Urban Structure.* New York: Random House, 1969.

Wilensly, Harold L., and Lebeaux, Charles N. *Industrial Society and Social Welfare.* New York: The Free Press, 1965.

Wirth, Louis. "Urbanism as a Way of Life." *American Journal of Sociology* 44 (July 1938): 1-24.

five

The Uses of Sociology

In 1962, the American Sociological Association commissioned three outstanding sociologists, Paul F. Lazarsfeld, William H. Sewell, and Harold L. Wilensky, to prepare a book on the theme "the uses of sociology." The book was to deal with where and how the sociological perspective and findings have made impact on the modern world. At a time when sociology was experiencing sudden new growth in popularity, sociologists seemed to be asking, "What earthly good is our discipline?" Have the steady stream of research projects, papers, books, meetings, and class-room lectures been of any practical use to government officials and industrial managers as well as the general populace as a whole? To answer these questions, and others like them, these three researchers responded with an edited volume 902 pages long, *The Uses of Sociology*.[1] Forty-three people contributed articles to the book. Touching upon almost every significant issue in modern living, the book argues persuasively for the practical utility of sociology to today's world.

For example, authors of various articles note that medical sociology can help in the cure and prevention of disease and may, therefore, contribute to a comprehensive health program. Diplomats and other foreign service personnel may be helped to understand the culture of the country in which they serve. Teachers, who teach in low-income areas, may benefit from sociological research in the field of education. Police contact with ethnic minorities may be improved and city planning enhanced by sociological study of the city. Sociologists may help in fertility control programs.

They may suggest helpful changes in the legal structure of society. Sociologists may serve as "expert witnesses" in some types of court cases or as consultants for federal, state, and local governments. Consumers may better understand their buying patterns because of sociologically oriented marketing research. Sociologists may serve as advisors to the military establishment in the areas of intelligence, psychological warfare, and the understanding of internal personnel management. They may also help government bodies to comprehend and influence foreign groups. Urban planning may be enhanced by sociological study. People concerned with such social problems as delinquency, divorce, unemployment, public health, aging, ethnic relationships, alcoholism, and drug abuse may profitably turn to sociologists for assistance in developing programs to alleviate human suffering in their respective areas.

The sociologist, we have seen, strives to acquire knowledge of human behavior in groups. While few would even claim more than a rudimentary stage of development in the discipline at this point, sociology is today "practical" enough to be of use in business, government, advertising, communications, administration, and a host of other areas of "real life." And the practicing sociologist is increasingly being employed in these contexts. As the principles of human behavior are discovered by all the social sciences in concert and as these principles are applied in various areas of life, it is hoped that a better, more humane world will develop.

But what about you? Your interests are probably in other areas of life and you have no intention of becoming a professional sociologist. As a nonsociologist, what can the study of sociology do for you? If you go beyond this brief introductory statement of sociological concern to study further the discipline of sociology, is there any practical and tangible outcome that you might reasonably expect? After all, don't you already know enough sociology? You are a member of society and, as such, participate daily in the very subject matter that sociology purports to study. Can't simple common sense serve to give you enough information about how people behave in groups? You are alive and you interact in groups every day. Are you not thereby a "sociologist"? Not at all. The study of sociology has much to offer the serious student. The following are among the things that you, as a nonsociologist, might hope to receive from pursuing further the study of this discipline.

Self-understanding

C. Wright Mills says in *The Sociological Imagination* that the task of sociology is to bring history and biography together.[2] Mills seems to mean that sociology should enable individuals to understand the historical forces that help to create events in their life. One should be able to interpret his or her own life more meaningfully in terms of social changes that occur about them. An excellent example of this aspect of sociological inquiry is Alvin Toffler's *Future Shock*.[3]

The serious student of sociology may be able to understand himself or herself better after, for example, a study of stratification. Family background, aspirations, or educational achievements (or nonachievements) may be more clearly understood by looking at the principles of stratification in our society. On the other hand, analysis of primary group interaction and changes in the family, occupational, and educational structure may help to explain alienation in the individual's experience of modern life. Few things could be more interesting than changes in family structure over the last forty years. This period of time represents the span during which most of the readers of this book, as well as their parents, grew up. Perceptive people may be more able to understand the agony of the so-called "generation gap" when this study is combined with information on reference groups.

The study of sociology assists one to understand values and attitudes. When consideration is given to the subculture in which one was reared and the various groups one participates in, one may be better able to analyze one's preferences as well as one's prejudices. The smug ethnocentrism and resultant provincialism of the easy acceptance of subcultural values and attitudes is greatly overcome when one realizes that the world is bigger than one's own backyard. As such, our world is expanded and we may more easily and comfortably find our places in it.

Finally, with reference to self-understanding, sociology may help us understand how we developed our particular personality. In *Individuals in Society,* James Kitchens and Leobardo Estrada call the chapter on personality development "The Path That Leads To You."[4] In interaction with other people and by internalizing the significant exchanges that occur in these events, we develop specific idiosyncrasies and patterns of response to stimuli. These experiences may properly be viewed as a pathway that develops and reveals the unique you.

When one begins to understand the social forces that help to shape human life, he or she is helped to cope with these factors. It seems that looking at social life from this perspective helps the individual to achieve a greater sense of control over his or her life. One's personal troubles may be reinterpreted in light of current events and contemporary social problems. While these perspectives do not in themselves ever completely explain the circumstances of the specific individual's life, they aid in throwing the light on what is occurring in that life.

Understanding Other People

A quick perusal of the outline of any good introductory sociology text reveals that sociology attempts to deal with the stuff of which life is made. No person exists for long without interaction with other people. Simply understanding the concepts of norms, roles, and positions goes a long way in explaining human behavior in a group. Much sociological reasoning is based upon the "function" of behavior. Of what specific utility is a certain behavior to the maintenance of a group or an event? For example, why do sporting events begin with the playing of the national anthem? Is more than a patriotic theme being played out? Is it merely a method of centering a large crowd's attention in preparation for the game? Or, why do most societies insist that marriage begin with a formal rite? Could it be that this ceremony is a public signal to the community that the couple involved is accepting the socially approved expectation, rights, and obligations associated with being married? When one approaches human behavior from this perspective, much light is shed on why people do the things they do.

Further, understanding other people's social backgrounds (as well as our own) helps us in dealing with them. Teachers confronted with a classroom full of children can profit by understanding the subculture from which a given child comes. Each one is more than an individual. Each is a bundle of social expectations acquired from parents, playmates, neighbors, and relatives. Coping with individual differences is made easier when one views the classroom from this perspective. And not only is coping made easier, but the teacher is more capable of helping the child to learn when he or she is aware of subcultural (as well as ethnic) differences. One may profit, therefore, by the study of race relations and urban sociology in this regard.

The study of social problems greatly enhances the individual's understanding of other people. One gains a picture of wide sections of society by looking at such subjects as alcoholism, drug abuse, mental illness, crime, alienation, and sexual deviance. These phenomena are set in a social context, and such social forces as technology, urbanization, and suburbanization are investigated for their impact upon the individual. The task of the sociologist as a scientist is simply to set forth the incidence and attempt to discover the possible causes of these phenomena. As the nonsociologist reads through these materials, however, something of the human misery and waste of human life associated with these social problems is perceived. You may be spurred to seek solutions in order to ameliorate the social conditions giving rise to such inhumane conditions of life.

Sociology, then, may help us to understand what makes other people tick. As we glean understanding of why people behave as they do, sociology may do nothing more than satisfy our curiosity. And, if it does no more, it has at least broadened our horizons. But it may also help create a greater tolerance for differences. In so doing, it may enable us to seek even further understanding of the life condition of other people. We may be helped to perceive structures of society that effectively block individuals from human fulfillment and, in so doing, drive us, if even in small ways, to seek solutions to these dehumanizing problems of life.

The Provision of Social Information

The study of sociology will teach you the precise definition of a host of commonly used words. Some of these are *alienation, institution, interaction, social change, crowds, rumors, community,* and *urban.* It is true that if you are to understand sociology you must know the sociological meaning of these terms. But it is equally as true that, if you understand these words, you are helped in interpreting your life and the social fabric that surrounds you.

In addition to the sociological jargon, sociology presents data about life that, when interpreted, reveals social conditions of great importance to American society. For example, consider a significant set of social statistics on black America. Blacks make up approximately 11 percent of our population. Approximately three-fourths of them live in cities and most in large cities. From 1960 to 1970, according to the U.S. Census Bureau, the black population increased in the U.S. by 3.8 million, and 3.2 million were born into the inner city. In comparison, the white population in that same period increased by 18.8 million, and 15.5 million were born in suburban areas. No more than 4.7 percent of the American suburban population was black in 1970; yet suburbia in 1970 accounted for 37 percent of our total population. These data are interesting for at least two reasons: (1) they indicate much about the condition of black life in the U.S. and the effect of social barriers that protects a predominately white suburban way of life, and (2) they reveal much about the condition of the city in American society. Washington, D.C., as an example, is over 71 percent black, but its suburbs contain less than 8 percent black residents.

Or, as another example, recall the section in the previous chapter on urbanization in the Third World. The phenomenal growth of urban centers in the largely rural developing nations reveals a devastating picture of human deprivation and misery. Statistics on population growth in these areas are even more alarming. As pessimistic as these figures are, no informed person should want to be ignorant of them. Nations on the other side of the globe are, in reality, as close as the next county and, because of the interdependence of the earth's nations, what occurs there has impact upon what occurs in the U.S. The price of oil in the Middle East helps determine the price of plastic in Japan that affects significantly the price of TVs in your friendly department store. By the same token, a drought in India affects the sale of grain the world over and may increase the price of the loaf of bread (and all other food) you will eat for breakfast tomorrow morning.

Beyond these kind of data, sociologists give us information and interpretation of other facts and figures. How many people are church members in the United States? Is the popularity of football declining? How many people own TVs and what effect does television viewing have on human behavior? The list of interesting and meaningful types of information that may be acquired from sociological study is virtually endless.

A Way of Looking at Life

All social sciences are concerned with the same basic phenomenon—human behavior. The intent of each is to shed light on what humans do and why they behave as they do. Differences among them lie not so much in their subject matter (although some disciplines do differ somewhat in this regard) as they do in their perspective. Each one approaches human behavior from its own vantage point, and together they present a composite picture of human activity. The anthropologist studies culture and social organization of primitive, prehistoric groups. The economist is concerned with how people acquire and spend their money. The political scientist asks questions about how humans govern themselves. The psychologist is concerned with the individual—his or her internal motivations and how he or she got that way. And sociologists are interested in group and the individual's interaction with others. They search to know how that interaction affects both the individual and the group.

There is, of course, some overlap in all the disciplines. The psychologist is, for example, not unaware of the social impact of interaction within the group. And, by the same token, the sociologist is cognizant of the affect of personality or individual internal factors in determining human activity. Again, the differences among the various disciplines lie in their starting points.

The study of sociology, therefore, adds another dimension to our understanding of human life by supplying us with a unique point of departure. The vantage point from which we view human behavior has been called the *sociological perspective,* the *sociological imagination,* or the *sociological dimension.* Its greatest strength lies in reminding us that people do not act in isolation. No person is an island. Each affects and is, in turn, affected by others. And each person brings to each behavioral context the composite of previous experiences through which he or she has lived.

One of the most potent concepts in this regard is W.I. Thomas's term *the definition of the situation.*[5] According to this concept, if a situation is defined as real, it is real in its consequences. That is, if I define, even against evidence, that a certain set of facts is true about a given situation, I act upon that definition. For me, the situation is real and thus the predefined consequences follow in due course. Studies have shown that, as an example, when teachers are told that their students are exceptionally bright, the students perform above average despite being normal children. It is also true that if I anticipate negative consequences in a given situation, negative consequences are much more likely to follow.

My expectations become, it seems, a "self-fulfilling prophecy." And when large numbers of people share the same definition of the situation, predefined expectations of necessity come true. If a significant number of people become convinced that the banks are about to fold and that everyone is rushing to the banks to withdraw their money, the result is a self-fulfilling prophecy. A bank "run" results and the banks do, in fact, fold.

You may acquire a way of looking at human life by the study of sociology. And this perspective is useful whether you are attempting to understand a national election, reading a short story, or trying to analyze the behavior of your children. You may be a biologist, homemaker, a lawyer, a teacher, or a business person. But, as an informed human, you will seek to understand the social phenomena that will surround you throughout life. Sociology represents a significant tool with which to satisfy your curiosity about how and why people act as they do. The sociological perspective is invaluable in treating disorders in society and in planning for better cities, schools, businesses, recreational outlets—in short, in creating a better, more humane world.

Summary

The intent of this chapter has been to present in brief fashion the practical uses of sociology for the nonsociologist. It was suggested that sociology is helpful to the informed social observer by aiding one to understand oneself and to comprehend the behavior of others, and by presenting a useful jargon and data relevant to how life is lived in today's world. Finally, sociology offers a useful perspective from which to analyze how and why people act as they do.

Notes

1. Paul F. Lazarsfeld, William H. Sewell, and Harold L. Wilensky, *The Uses of Sociology* (New York: Basic Books, Inc., 1967).
2. C. Wright Mills, *The Sociological Imagination* (New York: Oxford University Press, 1959), pp. 10-11.
3. Alvin Toffler, *Future Shock* (New York: Random House, 1970).
4. James A. Kitchens and Leobardo F. Estrada, *Individuals in Society: A Modern Introduction to Sociology* (Columbus, Ohio: Charles E. Merrill Publishing Co., 1974), pp. 63ff.
5. W.I. Thomas, *The Unadjusted Girl* (Boston: Little, Brown and Co., 1923), p. 42.

Additional Readings

Bierstedt, Robert. *The Social Order,* 3rd ed. New York: McGraw-Hill, 1970.

Mills, C. Wright. *The Sociological Imagination.* New York: Oxford University Press, 1959.

Toffler, Alvin. *Future Shock.* New York: Random House, 1970.

Wright, Jack, Jr., and Kitchens, James A. *Social Problems in America.* Columbus, Ohio: Charles E. Merrill Publishing Co., 1976.

six

Suggested Methods for Teachers

Raymond H. Muessig

Few sociologists have pursued "sociology for sociology's sake." Certainly curiosity about man, the intense desire to understand man, has always been a fundamental incentive to the most creative sociologists. I suspect that the quest for the key of knowledge that will unlock the mystery of one's own existence has been the profound inspiration of most great sociologists. Yet even these have rarely pursued sociology only to understand man or themselves. From its beginning sociology has been fundamentally concerned with solving the kinds of social problems that men inevitably and inadvertently create through their efforts to organize themselves in a complex, only partially understood world.... (Jack D. Douglas, The Relevance of Society)[1]

Introduction

Perhaps the word *relevance* has been overused and misused in recent years. *Relevance,* however, must still occupy a place in our spoken and written language, and the passage quoted above makes an important point. Facts, concepts, generalizations, topics, themes, and personal-social concerns related to all the social sciences can touch the lives of children and youth in elementary and secondary classrooms throughout the United States in manifold ways. And surely sociology is a field rich in pertinent ideas and germane problems worthy of study on a K-12 basis in forms adapted for different levels of maturity.

However, the very relevance of sociology—dealing as it often does with some of the most pressing, complex, delicate, and controversial issues in our society—imposes stringent instructional demands on teachers. Careful preparation and handling of vital sociological questions is required. But we social studies teachers can offer relevant aspects of sociology in increasingly interesting, meaningful, and enjoyable ways, and we can encourage and help our students to apply pertinent sociological insights to build a better tomorrow.

Helping Learners to Investigate the Socialization Process

In this book, Dr. Kitchens defines socialization as "the procedure by which the individual is taught the skills, attitudes, and values necessary for proper participation in his or her society." In *Sociology: Concepts and Characteristics,* Judson R. Landis writes that socialization is "the process whereby one learns and internalizes the norms and roles of the culture in which one lives."[2] And, in *Gender and Sex in Society,* Lucile Duberman discusses socialization as

> a process that allows the human animal to learn to live in his society according to its values. It permits him to develop a social self and to discover his status within the framework of his world. It is a process that encourages people to behave in ways that will gain social approval and the ability to predict the reactions their actions will evoke. Without socialization, society and humanness would disappear.[3]

Methodologically, socialization is an easy concept to introduce and to expand on a K-12 basis. In grades K-6, one need not use the word *socialization* in order to help children look at "things that we learn so we can get along with others." One of the major tasks for many five-year-olds, for example, is to grow from largely "me-centered" people to individuals who begin to adapt their behavior to others' needs, interests, problems, manners, rules, and laws. Senior high school students can employ the term *socialization* while considering nuances of peer group and/or larger societal expectations associated, say, with dating, going steady, trading rings or being "pinned," becoming engaged, and getting married.

The concept of socialization can be illustrated and vivified readily and appealingly at all grade levels through various uses of song lyrics, poems, short stories, novels, plays, films, newspaper and magazine articles and editorials, letters, personal accounts, diaries, memoirs, autobiographies, and biographies. For example, Barbara Robinson's delightfully funny novel *The Best Christmas Pageant Ever* might be read aloud to primary children and then discussed. It could be included on a shelf with related "socialization" books for intermediate pupils to read independently and to blend later into other related class activities. Here are a few passages that reveal something of the flavor of the novel:

> The Herdmans were absolutely the worst kids in the history of the world. They lied and stole and smoked cigars (even the girls) and talked dirty and hit little kids and cussed their teachers and took the name of the Lord in vain and set fire to Fred Shoemaker's old broken-down toolhouse.

> The Herdmans moved from grade to grade through the Woodrow Wilson School like those South American fish that strip your bones clean in three minutes flat... which was just about what they did to one teacher after another.

... The Herdmans were like most big families—the big ones taught the little ones everything they knew... and the proof of that was that the meanest Herdman of all was Gladys, the youngest.

We figured they were headed straight for hell, by way of the state penitentiary... until they got themselves mixed up with the church, and my mother, and our Christmas pageant.[4]

For grades 5-12, *Pistol* by Adrienne Richard contains excellent examples of the socialization process at work, such as the following:

As we rode, I studied Tom and everything about him. How he wore his hat, how he tied his jumper jacket to the back of his saddle, how he rode, how he took the jounce of his horse on the balls of his feet, in the knees and in the shoulders, how he stood in the stirrups with the reins held almost over the horse's ears when he wanted a fast trot. To me he was the ideal cowman ....

... When five yearling steers took off in five different directions, I wondered if I'd ever learn. When I brought a bunch in to the main herd and saw Tom, I knew that if I kept on watching him, I would learn everything I needed to know.

...Tom never ridiculed me. He never cussed me out the way Red did. He didn't say much of anything, but he let me know that I could make it and I would.[5]

Prior to using Louise Fitzhugh's *Nobody's Family Is Going to Change* to focus on an especially important, potentially controversial, and immensely discussable dimension of the socialization process with fifth to ninth graders, the teacher might find it helpful to read this selection from Duberman's *Gender and Sex in Society:*

A social role is attached to one's sex status, as roles are attached to all statuses. Here I shall refer to this as one's *gender role,* meaning the socially learned patterns of behavior that differentiate men from women in a given society. Masculinity and feminity are gender roles, acquired during one's lifetime through learning, role-taking, imitation, observation, and direct instruction. ...

A society decides what is considered masculine and what feminine, and the individual interprets these decisions and applies them to him- or herself. Gender, then, is learned behavior, usually related to one's sex, but sex status does not necessarily determine gender role. One's degree of proficiency in playing one's gender role depends on how well one has been socialized, how much one seeks approval from society, and how much one's gender-role performance has been reinforced with positive sanctions.[6]

The teacher might paraphrase, digest, and read aloud to students his or her version of the preceding passage, answer questions regarding key terms, share the material below, and then open a longer exchange of ideas followed by research independently and in small groups.

"What's funny about being a lawyer?"

"It's not that being a lawyer is funny. It's the idea of you as a lawyer. Why in the world would you want to do that?"

"You think I'm too stupid?" Emma found she was holding her breath....

"Of course you're not stupid. You get straight A's in school. It's the *life* of a lawyer. I think you're too young to realize that the life of a lawyer is very rough. If you knew more about it, I don't think you'd choose it. I don't think you'd be thinking about it at all."

"What would I choose?" . . .

"I think you'd choose marrying a man you loved, marrying a lawyer perhaps, and raising two lovely children—"[7]

Scott O'Dell's *Carlota* could be used nicely in conjunction with *Nobody's Family Is Going to Change* at the same grade levels.

. . ."You have raised Carlota as a vaquero. She thinks of nothing but horses. . . . "

What she said was true. I *had* been raised as a vaquero. I had been taught to do everything a horseman could do. My father had even named me after his son, Carlos, who had been killed by the Piutes.[8]

No More School by Howard S. Rowland is a nonfiction personal account which provides a solid example of the socialization process in action. The junior high school teacher could read aloud from this source to a class, and the senior high school teacher might recommend the book to motivated individual students who read well.

No More School is an account of how my wife and I attempted to give our children a fresh start, to remove them from contemporary middle-class, TV-oriented, peer-group dominated, suburban American life—particularly from that unnatural children's society called school—and allow each of them to discover whatever it was he wanted and could get out of being alive.

The book covers a ten-month period from November 1969 to September 1970. The place, for the most part is La Herradura, a remote fishing village in Spain, where we settled down with one thing in mind—a determination to free our children of teachers, textbooks, classrooms, and routines.

When it was time to return to the States, to Westchester County and the Lakeland schools, the Rowland family was a tight and stable society. . . . [9]

Autobiography provides one of the best means for helping learners in the elementary and secondary grades to investigate what the socialization process can do to and for individuals. The following three examples are, respectively, from *The Story of My Life* by Clarence Darrow, *My Life* by Golda Meir, and *Nigger: An Autobiography* by Dick Gregory with Robert Lipsyte:

. . . I began at the primer and read over and over the McGuffey readers, up to the sixth, while at the district school. . . . I am sure that no set of books ever came from any press that was so packed with love and righteousness as were those readers. Their religious and ethical stories seem silly now, but at that time it never occurred to me that those tales were utterly impossible lies which average children should easily have seen through.

. . . (M)y home was well supplied with books, and my father was eager that all of us should learn. He watched our studies with the greatest care and diligently elaborated and supplemented whatever we absorbed in school. . . .

Schools were not established to teach and encourage the pupil to think; beyond furnishing a place for keeping the children out of the way, their effort was to cement the minds of pupils according to certain moulds. The teachers were employed to teach the truth, and the most important truth concerned the salvation of their souls. From the first grade to the end of the college course they were taught not to think, and the instructor who dared to utter anything in conflict with ordinary beliefs and customs was promptly dismissed, if not destroyed. Even now there are very few schools that encourage the young or the old to think out questions for themselves. And yet, life is a continuous problem for the living, and first of all we should be equipped to think, if possible. . . . [10]

It was not a pleasure trip, that fourteen-day journey aboard ship. . . . Mother, Sheyna and Zipke were seasick most of the time, but I felt well and can remember staring at the sea for hours, wondering what Milwaukee would be like. The ship was packed with immigrants from Russia — pale, exhausted and just as scared as we were. . . .

My father met us in Milwaukee, and he seemed changed: beardless, American-looking, in fact a stranger. . . .

. . . [O]n the morning after our arrival he determinedly marched all of us downtown on a shopping expedition. He was horrified, he said, by our appearance. We looked so dowdy and "Old World," particularly Sheyna in her matronly black dress. He insisted on buying us all new clothes, as though by dressing us differently he could turn us, within twenty-four hours, into three American-looking girls. . . .

. . . In his own eyes, he was on the way to becoming a full-fledged American Jew, and he liked it.

I started school in a huge, fortresslike building on Fourth Street near Milwaukee's famous Schlitz beer factory, and I loved it. I can't remember how long it took me to learn English . . . , but I have no recollection of the language ever being a real problem for me, so I must have picked it up quickly. . . .

. . . I think back on those five years in Milwaukee with great pleasure. There was so much to see and do and learn that the memory of Pinsk was almost erased. . . . In September, when we had been in America just over three months, my father told us to be sure and watch the famous Labor Day parade in which he, too, would be marching. . . . [F]or me, that parade — the crowds, the brass bands, the floats, the smell of popcorn and hot dogs — symbolized American freedom. . . . [11]

There were other fathers along the way, men who reached out and gave me their hands. There was Mister Coleman, principal of the Cote Brilliant Grammar School where I was transferred when I was thirteen. He called me into his office once when I was in the seventh grade. I walked right up to his big oak desk, and he leaned back in his swivel chair and looked me up and down.

"I've got a problem you might be able to help me with, Richard. It's about your job as a patrol boy."

"Sure, Mister Coleman."

"I've had complaints about how rough you are at the school crossing, Richard. You push the students, you use bad language. Now, I've watched you, Richard, and I know you're one of our best patrol captains. You don't let anybody cross until all the cars have stopped, you get right out there and make those trucks stay behind the white line. I don't want to have to take your badge away."

"Well, Mister Coleman . . ."

"How old are you, Richard?"

"Fourteen." I was embarrassed at being behind.

"You're a leader, Richard, a smart boy, a little older than some of the other students. They'll do just what you tell them if you're kind and strong. You've got to help them out on that corner, you can't be hateful. You're just like a father with a lot of children to watch after. Now go out there and keep those little kids safe.''

At three o'clock I ran out on my post and stood out there like a happy traffic cop, as straight as a man could stand, proud because everybody was looking at me, because kids couldn't cross the street without me. Milkmen, laundrymen, they'd pull up their trucks and I'd make sure all the kids were on the sidewalk before I'd wave them through. The drivers would lean out and wave at me and call hello as they passed by. I was somebody.[12]

Finally, the teacher could read aloud selections from appropriate biographies to a class and/or might assist each learner in grades 5-12 in locating an enlightening biography. Mary Kay Phelan's *Probing the Unknown: The Story of Dr. Florence Sabin* and Leslie Alexander Lacy's *Cheer the Lonesome Traveler: The Life of W. E. B. Du Bois* should serve as examples here:

The girls were chatting in small groups when President Seelye called them together for a few informal remarks. He wanted to emphasize, he said, that Smith College had never published any set rules of behavior. The young ladies were simply expected to observe "the unwritten code of a good society." . . .[13]

W. E. B. Du Bois had a typical Great Barrington [Massachusetts] boyhood... Young Will Du Bois absorbed the Yankee culture very well. In fact he was quite thoroughly New England....

...Strongly influenced by the prevailing social thoughts during his boyhood, he believed that anyone willing to work could earn a living; those with wealth and influence deserved it, and poverty and crime were the results of laziness and immorality. His attitude about immigrants was typical: they would be all right once they became properly Americanized.

Later the man from Great Barrington would question the values he learned as a boy, but until he finished high school Du Bois was a perfect product of his environment....[14]

After elementary and secondary learners have gained some familiarity with facets of the socialization process through fictional and nonfictional examples, the teacher might move into a procedure that can be adapted easily for use on a K-12 basis. The adaptability feature of this approach will be demonstrated here with a suggestion for the kindergarten and with a recommendation for the twelfth grade. Innumerable possibilities at other grade levels should suggest themselves to you.

Thirty years ago, as a journalism major enrolled in a newspaper reporting course, I was taught to try to include the *four* or *five Ws* —Who, What, When, Where, and sometimes *Why*—in the lead paragraph of a story. Similarly, the elementary or secondary social studies teacher could introduce class members to the 5 *Ws* of the socialization process. *Who,* of course, would focus on those being socialized and those doing the socializing. Recipients might include a baby, a young child, a child, an adolescent, etc., on up through a very old person. A mother, a father, a grandparent, a sister, a brother, an aunt, an uncle, a friend, a teacher, a classmate, a minister, a priest, a rabbi, a youth organization leader, a driving instructor, a police officer, a plant supervisor, a labor organization representative, a corporation executive, a wife, a husband, etc., might be studied in various ways as an individual agent of socialization. Institutional agents of socialization could include the family, the school, the church, the synagogue, the mass media, the different levels of government, and so on. Expectations, habits, skills, manners, rules, regulations, laws, morals, opinions, attitudes, appreciations, beliefs, values, and the like might comprise the *what* into which children and youth could inquire. *When* obviously concerns the frequent times in the life of an individual during which socialization takes place. Through a number of classroom experiences, girls and boys, young women and men might discover that the *where* of socialization can range from the kitchenette to the banquet hall, the sidewalk to the turnpike, the playground to the coliseum, the kindergarten teacher's lap to the university professor's auditorium, the folding chair in a Sunday school classroom to the bench of a choir loft in a great cathedral. And, elementary and secondary learners may find that the *why* of socialization runs the gamut from "just because" to "the will of God."

The kindergarten teacher might introduce his or her pupils to the 5 *W*s of the socialization process by using discussion pictures mounted on heavy cardboard and placed along the classroom chalk ledges. Already mounted photographs could be selected from commercial collections, such as the Harper & Row *Discussion Pictures for Beginning Social Studies.*[15] And/or photographs found in newspapers and magazines might be cut out and mounted. And/or the teacher could draw stick figures or other pictures right on posterboard. In any event, illustrations might show younger children engaged in different activities in various places, such as

> looking out for cars before crossing a street,
> hanging a coat on a classroom coatrack hook,
> whistling,
> putting on rubber boots,
> taking a dog for a walk,
> sharing classroom materials or equipment,
> skipping,
> shaking hands,
> tying shoes,
> returning something to its proper place in the home or the school,
> coloring,
> painting,
> asking for the help of a policeofficer or a block parent,
> dividing an orange with someone,
> dialing a telephone,
> reading a word printed by a teacher on a chalkboard or an experience chart,
> playing an instrument in a rhythm band,
> feeding a kitten,
> washing hands,
> meeting a visitor at the classroom door,
> saying grace at a meal,
> brushing teeth.

Prior to leading a class discussion, the kindergarten teacher might encourage pupils to look at the pictorial display during appropriate times for a few days, both as a means for arousing class members' interest and making it possible for the boys and girls to study details in the illustrations, especially the smaller pictures. Then, depending on children's responses to the 5 *W*s activity and their attention spans, the teacher could invite a discussion of one or more of the learners' favorite photographs each day for perhaps a week. To launch this approach, the teacher might ask, "Would one of you like to choose a picture for us to talk about?" A child would then select an illustration. He or she could place a larger drawing on an easel in front of the group. The child might move slowly from one classmate to another so each person could examine a smaller photograph. Next, pointing to the illustration on the easel or holding a picture so it can be viewed by individuals in the class, the teacher might ask questions such as the following:

Who is in this picture?	The teacher would help the children to identify each person in the illustration. A pupil might say, "I see a little girl." Or, "That's a boy and his daddy." (Or his big sister or his teacher or a firefighter, etc.)
What is happening in this picture?	The teacher would encourage learners to describe the action observed in the photograph and to enlarge on their descriptions. One class member, for example, might say, "Santa is talking to a little boy in his lap." Another child might elaborate.
When might this be happening?	Obviously the kindergarten teacher does not expect five-year-olds to have a sophisticated sense of chronological sequence in general and dates in particular. However, some of the children might respond in this manner: 'When you are little." "Before you go to school." "Pretty soon." "When you are in the first grade." "When you get bigger."
Where could this be happening?	Again, the kindergarten teacher would anticipate brief, uncomplicated replies from his or her little ones. "At home." "In Sunday school." "Here. In kindergarten." "On a farm."
Why might this be happening?	At first, the *why* of the socialization process might be difficult for many kindergartners, and the teacher could find it necessary to help the class with hints, additional questions, and specific examples. In time, however, pupils might make contributions similar to these: " 'Cause the little boy could get hit by a car if he doesn't listen to the crosswalk lady and wait for a green light to go across the street." "Ummm, the teacher is helping every boy and girl learn their name and address and phone number so they can tell somebody—like a policeman—if they get lost." "If you don't brush your teeth, they'll smell bad and fall out. That's why the school nurse in the picture is showing the kids how to brush right."

As a means of encouraging individual high school seniors to apply their understanding of the 5 Ws of the socialization process, the secondary social studies teacher might ask each class member to complete two copies of a form such as figure 1.

The 5 Ws of the Socialization Process				
Who	What	When	Where	Why

Figure 1.

In the "Who" column of the first copy of the teacher-prepared form, every participant would record the names of five agents of socialization—a father (I. M. Older, Jr.), a grandfather (I. M. Older, Sr.), a teacher (Shirley Smarter), a coach (Reel E. Bigger), and a summer employer (Definite Lee Richer), for example—who have played important parts in the student's life. In the "What" column of the first copy of the handout, each twelfth grader would enter skills, attitudes, values, etc., transmitted by the agents of socialization. For instance, adjacent to and horizontal with the name of Reel E. Bigger in the "What" column, the learner might write, "Mr. Bigger, my coach, has taught me that winning is important in football and in life, but playing hard and fair also count for a lot." The "When," "Where," and "Why" sections would be completed in a similar fashion.

In the second copy of the form, each senior in the social studies class would think about herself or himself as an agent of socialization. In the "Who" column of the second copy, therefore, the young adult would write in the names of five people whom she or he has socialized and their connection with the writer (younger brother, pupil in the author's Sunday school class, etc.) and then continue with a "What," a "When," a "Where," and a "Why" matched to each name.

After the teacher has received two completed copies of the form from all participants, he or she might prepare two large bulletin board displays patterned after the design of the handout. The first display might be entitled "Looking at Others As Agents of Socialization." Actual names of people found in students' copies of the handout would not be used in the bulletin board display. Rather, the teacher would employ words such as *Mothers, Guidance Counselors,* and *Ministers* as general headings in the "Who" column and would combine and abstract data matching these general headings from pertinent ideas submitted by learners. Thus, there might be 15-20 entries, say, in the "What," "When," "Where," and "Why" columns matched horizontally with the word *Teacher.* The second display could be entitled "Looking at Ourselves As Agents of Socialization." Again, real names would not appear. General headings (*Younger Sisters, Nieces, Cousins, Friends,* etc.) for those people for whom class members served as agents of socialization would serve in the "Who" column to contain matching lists in other columns.

Prior to what should be a stimulating and meaningful class discussion, the high school seniors would study the two bulletin board displays carefully at appropriate times for several days. There could be considerable interest and interaction as alert students call attention in particular to such things as inconsistencies in expectations in the "What" column or incompatibilities in reasons in the "Why" category.

Of course, an approach such as the preceding could motivate eager twelfth graders to propose various follow-up activities suggested by topics, themes, problems, and controversial issues tied to the 5 *W*s of the socialization process. Or, the teacher herself or himself might catch something said during the class discussion that could be suitable for an in-depth, postscript inquiry. Although "manners" might seem like an absolutely deadly topic for seventeen-year-olds at first blush, a bright teacher with a sense of humor and a responsive group could help learners to gain some unique insights and to have some fun through an examination of this dimension of socialization. (I have written this methodological suggestion for seniors, but a study of selected manners could be conducted easily on a K-12 basis.)

The teacher might introduce an investigation of manners by reading passages such as these from a cover story entitled "America's New Manners," which appeared in *Time* in November of 1978:

> ... It has become extremely complicated to be polite in America....
>
> ... To this last half-generation, manners were sexist, hypocritical, emotionally invalid or, at last, hopelessly and rather touchingly quaint. The women's movement called a world of once reflexive rituals into doubt. The masculine urge to rise when a woman entered the room seemed a sort of humiliating impulse, uncontrollable, incontinent. A man seated on the downtown bus might endure agonies of self-examination before offering his seat to a woman. The male had to learn to size up the female by age, education and possible ferocity of feminism before opening a door for her: Would the courtesy offend her? It made for ambiguity: If a man studiously refuses to open the door for a woman, is he sexually liberated? Or just an ill-bred slob?
>
> The question of the unmarried couple is everywhere. How to handle the linguistic problem of what to call the person with whom one's daughter lives? "Lover" is too archaically lubricious by a shade or two. "Roommate" sounds like a freshman dorm. "Bedmate" is too sexually specific, but "Friend" is too sweetly platonic. "Boyfriend" and "girlfriend" are a bit adolescent. "Partner" sounds as if they run a hardware store together. The Census Bureau calls them "Partners of the Opposite Sex Sharing Living Quarters."...[16]

At the start the twelfth-grade social studies teacher could read aloud to the class from a recent book on the 5 *W*s of manners by an avowed authority, or agent of socialization in the "Who" column. The following are illustrative excerpts from *The Amy Vanderbilt Complete Book of Etiquette: A Guide to Contemporary Living: Revised and Expanded by Letitia Baldrige,* published in 1978:

> ..."Etiquette" is a starchy word, but manners are not starchy. Etiquette has to do with when you wear white gloves and how you unfold the napkin on your lap; *real manners*

are being thoughtful toward others, being creative in doing nice things for others, or sympathizing with others' problems. There is nothing formal or stiff about that!

As our population grows and we are forced to live ever more closely together, never have manners been more desperately needed. But as daily life becomes more complicated, we also have more options than ever before....

This book is really an "exercise in options," because fortunately the hidebound rules of behavior have relaxed. One may do "this" or perhaps "that" and be correct. What has not changed is the need for consideration of others. For this, there are no options.

Teen-agers, especially in recent years, feel that they inhabit a world of their own in which they can make their own rules. ...

Every teen-ager needs to be reminded about many of the things that careful adults take for granted, such as the need to answer all invitations promptly, to acknowledge gifts graciously and quickly, to show respect and courtesy toward adults, to be protective and kindly toward the younger and weaker.[17]

As an enrichment activity, the teacher might encourage interested students to compare recommendations on some specifics of manners in the 1978 revision and enlargement of the Vanderbilt with the original edition of 1952. Able, serious, budding scholars could also compare selected current manners with given polite standards in past centuries in U.S. and in other societies, while keeping the 5 Ws of the socialization process in mind. However, the following paragraphs describe a strategy likely to appeal and to work with an entire twelfth-grade class.

First, the teacher would distribute five 4"× 6" lined cards to every class member and ask students to compose 1-5 questions regarding manners, using a separate card to record each question. Here are some examples of questions that could be asked:

1. A senior girl wants to attend the prom. A guy she doesn't really like asks her. She says OK so she won't have to stay home. Two days later a boy she likes asks her. What should she do?

2. A graduating senior girl wants to go to the prom. No one has asked her. Is it all right for her to ask a fellow in her class? In the junior class? From another school? Her brother? A cousin?

3. A senior's parents send out a bunch of graduation announcements to relatives and friends, and he gets alot of presents. He flunks a course, so he can't graduate. What's he supposed to do about the announcements and presents?

4. At a high school spaghetti dinner given for graduating seniors, is it OK for students to tuck their napkins up under their chins to protect their clothes?

5. At a graduation buffet dinner party, who should serve himself or herself first—a boy, a girl, a teenage boy, a teenage girl, a man, or a woman?

6. The parents of a graduating senior give him a new 5-speed bicycle to use when he goes to college. He would like to have a 10-speed bike or to use the money toward the purchase of a car or something else. Should he talk to his folks?

7. A seventeen-year-old guy wants to impress a girl on a first date. He takes her to a flick, where he buys a big box of popcorn and two Cokes. After they leave

the theater, he looks at the gas gauge and sees that he needs gas. So he stops and buys $4 worth. At a pizza place, he is getting ready to order. He just happens to look in his wallet. He finds out that he doesn't have enough money to pay for a pizza. What should he do?

Second, one person in the class would walk around the room, gather all the questions in a cardboard box, shake the cards in the box, walk around the room a second time, and allow everyone to draw one question out of the box. Third, on the back, unlined side of the 4"× 6" card, each student would answer the question he or she has drawn. Fourth, the cards would be gathered in the cardboard box again, shaken, and handed in the box to the teacher. Fifth, the teacher would read aloud to the group both the question and the answer on each card, thus protecting the identity of all participants in the teaching strategy. Sixth, the teacher could announce the creation of a "Dear Ecivda" advice column on manners, for which he or she would serve as the editor. The teacher might go through the question cards remaining in the cardboard box, selecting the most interesting, humorous, important, difficult, varied, and/or frequent questions, combining related problems into single queries, and then writing a series of "letters" to "Dear Ecivda." Each letter would focus on a single concern with respect to manners and would be placed in an "In" basket on the teacher's desk. Seventh, motivated individual students could read through the letters, pick given letters to which they would like to reply, write letters offering advice on manners, staple their answers to the questions, and place their contributions in an "Out" basket on the teacher's desk. Eighth, the teacher would type the best question-answer combinations on fluid duplicator masters and "publish" a "Dear Ecivda" column daily for a week. Each column might contain 3-5 questions and answers in a "Dear Ecivda"-"Dear Troubled" format. Ninth, at the start of the period each day for the week, each senior would receive a copy of the column "hot off the press," read the questions and answers, and have an opportunity to ask further questions and/or to offer his or her reactions.

Tenth, the teacher might give the class some practice in inductive thinking. Using questions and answers on manners as particulars, twelfth-graders could endeavor to assemble some general statements about their manners and those of others in American society. For example, one student might offer comments such as these in a class discussion:

"I'm just thinking out loud, O.K.? I don't want you to take me the wrong way and to come down on top of me. But let me try a few things that seem to be good manners and then see if they add up to something."

"Newlyweds are supposed to send a thank you note for each wedding gift they receive. Right? And they are expected to do this even if they don't need the present or like it. Or, even if they don't know what it is! Now, I know that we say, 'It isn't the gift; it's the thought behind it that counts.' But that's not always right either, is it? Don't a lot of people give presents to people they don't know or like very well for a lot of wrong reasons? I mean, like you give the couple a gift 'cause you're obligated to the bride's father in business or something, huh?"

"Or, what about a clerk in a store? Let's say that a customer is being really nasty ... or critical ... or unfair. That sort of stuff. But the clerk stands there and smiles ... and thanks the customer for the criticisms, even though they are stupid or they hurt."

"And, let's say that your husband or your wife has died. You are really depressed and tired. But you have to send out a whole bunch of notes to people who sent cards and came to the funeral. Maybe you got a letter from a lady who was nosy or even cruel. But you have to thank her anyway."

"Or, a girl you know gets her hair fixed a new way. Now she looks like Orphan Annie. But you tell her that it makes her look great."

"Now, doesn't it seem to you guys that a lot of the things we do are phony? I saw a sign on a wall or a desk or someplace one time that said something like, 'Always be sincere, whether you mean it or not.' Could that idea be part of our system of manners and even our whole society?"

Inductive thinking skills that twelfth graders have improved while forming particulars regarding manners into generalizations could be readily transferred into such areas as rules, regulations, laws, and values. Having formed generalizations about manners, rules, regulations, laws, and values, then, students could use those generalizations as particulars leading to even higher-level generalizations about the 5 Ws of the socialization process.

I have one additional set of methodological suggestions to help learners to investigate the socialization process. In chapter 2, Professor Kitchens discusses desocialization and anticipatory socialization, defining the former as "the process of unlearning behaviors that are acceptable at earlier stages of life" and the latter as "learning about expected behavior prior to entering a new social position."

In the primary grades—without using the terms *desocialization* and *anticipatory socialization,* of course—the teacher can easily give young children a feeling for the general idea these words represent. Having made prior arrangements, the teacher might walk with his or her charges to a neighborhood bicycle shop, where a tricycle, a sidewalk (convertible) bicycle with training wheels, a sidewalk bicycle without its training wheels, and a full-sized bicycle would be lined up on display. With little difficulty, primary children could observe that a tricycle helps prepare a child to ride a sidewalk bicycle with training wheels (which *is* a kind of tricycle); that a sidewalk bicycle with training wheels becomes a bicycle as the side wheels are raised and discarded in time; and that the small sidewalk bicycle gets a boy or girl ready to handle a full-sized bicycle. Learning to do without the side wheels on a tricycle or a sidewalk bicycle with training wheels involves "unlearning" or "desocialization," be the example ever so humble. The purchase of a sidewalk bicycle illustrates "anticipatory socialization" beautifully, for parents know that they will be removing the training wheels so the art of balancing a two-wheeled bicycle can be mastered. Later, in the classroom, the teacher can encourage pupils to discuss things they learned at home that helped them to get ready to go to nursery school, experiences they had in nursery school which prepared them for kindergarten, and so on, right up to their current grade level, including third graders. The teacher would then repeat the home-nursery school-kindergarten-first grade-etc., sequence, this time focusing discussion on things class members used to know and do that have been forgotten or abandoned. Getting along without a nap is one of many examples which boys and girls might mention.

On a K-12 basis, short stories and novels illustrative of desocialization and anticipatory socialization abound. In Betty Baker's *Killer-of-Death,* for instance, both the shaman's son and the protagonist leave childhood and are initiated into adulthood.

... "Where is the shaman's son?"

"He left for the dry country two days ago."

In twelve days he'd return, proving that he could find food and water in the desert as well as any warrior. Then, after serving on three raids, he'd be a warrior himself. . . .

I slept well and woke next morning eager to be on my way. The family gathered to see me leave. . . .

I checked myself again to be sure I'd forgotten nothing. Quiver, bow case and bow. Knife in my moccasin top, a bone awl for mending the moccasins, a fire drill and my medicine bag. No food and no water. All was ready.

My father blew hoddentin to the Four Directions. My mother pressed a piece of turquoise into my hand. The blue stone was the strongest of medicines. Silently I turned away. Atop the last rise I looked back. They were still watching. Smiling, I trotted into the canyon. The sentry rose to stand against the sky and lift his rifle in farewell. He was the last person I was to see for fourteen days.[18]

After reading passages from various stories and novels aloud for class discussion and assisting children and youth to find pertinent publications for independent reading, the teacher in grades 5-12 could ask learners to discuss and/or to write a paragraph or two in response to this familiar quotation from I Corinthians 13: 11, which is really appropriate for the purpose envisioned here and which has been written for easier understanding:

... When I was a child, I spoke as a child. I understood as a child, I thought as a child; but when I became a man, I gave up the ways of a child. . . .

With senior high school students, the teacher might lead into various activities related to desocialization and anticipatory socialization by reading aloud to the class from sociological works, such as *Female & Male: Socialization, Social Roles, and Social Structure* by Clarice Stasz Stoll, and popular lay sources, such as *Passages: Predictable Crises of Adult Life* by Gail Sheehy.

Socialization . . . is a lifelong process, for individuals move through many settings and relationships as they age, each with its special demands and requirements. Whenever a woman enters the work force or a man becomes a father, each must learn new tasks, attitudes, and shift from past preferences and behaviors to new ones. The process can be more subtle, an example being the shifts in age situs from youth to adulthood through middle age to old age. . . .[19]

... The more I interviewed, the more I noticed similarities in the turning points people described. . . .

Before 18, the motto is loud and clear: "I have to get away from my parents." But the words are seldom connected to action. . . .

After 18, we begin Pulling Up Roots in earnest. College, military service, and short-term travels are all customary vehicles our society provides for the first round trips between family and a base of one's own. In the attempt to separate our view of the world from our family's view, despite vigorous protestations to the contrary—"I know exactly what I want!"—we cast about for any beliefs we can call our own. And in the process of testing those beliefs we are often drawn to fads, preferably those most mysterious and inaccessible to our parents.

Learning to cross the street is comparatively easy. Coming to trust our own judgment in volatile matters such as sex, intimacy, competition, the choice of friends, loves, career, ideology, and the right values to pursue is a much longer and more demanding process.[20]

Encouraging Children and Youth to Consider the Concept of Norms

As a means of setting the stage for this portion of the chapter, a review of some of Dr. Kitchens' treatment of norms in the second chapter is useful. Kitchens has written that norms may be defined simply as shared behavioral expectations. They are the rules of appropriate behavior shared by those persons interacting, and they are a part of virtually every human exchange. Norms help make for stable and orderly arrangements among groups of interacting individuals. They keep individuals from having to undergo the problems of enacting rules in each new situation and make orderly transition from one generation to the next.

Another helpful analysis is this passage from the "Introduction: The Sociology of Social Problems" to *Social Problems: The Contemporary Debates,* written by John B. Williamson, Jerry F. Boren, and Linda Evans:

> Social behavior is strongly influenced by social norms (rules). Some of these norms are formalized as laws, and sanctions (punishments) for violations are formally codified. But most social norms take the form of informal behavioral expectations. Although the sanctions for violations of these expectations are informal, they can be just as effective as any legal statute. When someone appears at a public function in entirely inappropriate attire, speaks to a superior without the proper degree of respect, or shows too much affection for the spouse of a friend, there will be sanctions. The sanction may be a raised eyebrow, or social rejection by the community that may last for years. These informal behavioral expectations are generally internalized without question. They are the customary or natural way things are done. . . . [21]

A meaningful study of the useful and comprehensive idea of norms in grades K-12 can serve innumerable purposes. Theoretically, an investigation related to norms could foster a subject-centered, a citizenship, an emergent needs, a social functions, a reflective, a structure-of-the-disciplines, an inquiry, a values clarification, a moral education, or some other perspective, or a combination thereof. A blending might occur, for example, if the teacher were to use inquiry strategies to help learners arrive at a structure-of-the-disciplines concept of norms integrated into the reflective consideration of normative issues.

There are countless ways in which elementary and secondary teachers could use novels, written for children, adolescents, and adults, to involve learners in a study of norms. Through novels, they could learn a great deal about the nature of norms, consistencies and inconsistencies in norms in different contexts ranging from personal through global levels, and difficulties associated with clarifying values and warranting beliefs pertinent to norms accepted and rejected.

The elementary or secondary teacher, for instance, might begin each Monday the first month of the school year with her or his normative, belief-oriented "Quotation of the Week," which could appear on the chalkboard in the front of the classroom, on a long strip of butcher paper taped above the chalkboard, or on reproduced slips of paper (one for each learner). The quotation from a novel could simply restate a societal behavioral expectation, or it might endorse or reject, affirm or oppose, or praise or ridicule some rule of appropriate behavior. The literary excerpt could view a norm from a perspective that is optimistic or pessimistic, serious or humorous, profound or shallow, sincere or trifling. It might represent the teacher's conviction one Monday but not another. But the passage should provoke some kind of reaction in a total-class discussion, in small-group interaction sessions, in independent position statements, posters, cartoons, banners, and the like.

During a second month, the teacher could invite all of her or his charges to "enter a contest for the 'Quotation of the Week.'" At this stage, pupils could submit selections they like from novels that appeal to them. The teacher would be the sole judge and would choose a weekly normative assertion which class members would then contemplate. The winners of the second month's contest would be the judges who would identify the best four or five quotations entered by their classmates, and the winning passages would be displayed afresh each Monday of the third month. Next, by drawing slips of paper numbered from 1-4 or 1-5, participants would form into four or five committees. Each committee would decide on its own fictional quotation for one Monday of the fourth month and would letter and illustrate a bulletin board display. The following months everyone in the class would be encouraged to choose from appropriate novels excerpts expressing views of norms, which might appear on a variety of creative visuals, such as collages and mobiles.

In any event, the following are but a few of the kinds of normative quotations from novels that might be used for learners' deliberations:

...The world is not nice to good people.... (*My Name Is Asher* by Chaim Potok)[22]

...There isn't any better defence against life than a sense of humor.... (*Grover* by Vera and Bill Cleaver)[23]

...Ain't nobody in this world that's as good as he'd like people to think he is. (*The Seige of Silent Henry* by Lynn Hall)[24]

Use people or people will use you.
Let anyone need you, but never need anyone.
Don't sit back. Stand up and take, grab, get, get your share of what there is to get from life.(*When the Sad One Comes to Stay* by Florence Parry Heide)[25]

...I decided that when I grew up I would be very careful not to get in the habit of thinking only of my own happiness. There were too many things in the world that weren't right, and it would be wrong for me to live my life as if they didn't exist. (*The Two of Us* by Claude Berri)[26]

...A person's got to think, otherwise that person's no better than a trained seal balancing a ball on his nose.... (*Summer of My German Soldier* by Bette Greene)[27]

...What is a man? A man does what he wants to do, and if he does it well, ain't nobody going to say he ain't a man....(*Nobody's Family Is Going to Change* by Louise Fitzhugh)[28]

...I figure it's up to each of us to make up his or her mind and then stick with it until proven wrong.... (*Sunday Father* by John Neufeld)[29]

...The only thing you can't be free from is the consequence of what you do....(*The Man Without a Face* by Isabelle Holland)[30]

The point of playing a game is to win.... Otherwise, what on earth is the use?...Defeat is numbing.... Defeat is humbling, obscene. (*His Enemy, His Friend* by John R. Tunis)[31]

. . . It is well, when in difficulties, to say never a word, neither black nor white. Speech is silver but silence is golden. . . . (*The Prime of Miss Jean Brodie* by Muriel Spark)[32]

How strange it is that people of honest feelings and sensibility, who would not take advantage of a man born without arms or legs or eyes—how such people think nothing of abusing a man born with low intelligence. . . . (*Flowers for Algemon* by Daniel Keyes)[33]

. . . The only babies that should be brought into the world are babies that are wanted. Otherwise it is misery for the child, for the mother, for countless numbers of people. . . . (*Growing Up in a Hurry* by Winifred Madison)[34]

. . . [I]t is unfortunate that the law requires everyone to attend school up to age seventeen. It means that those . . . who are trying to learn something are interfered with all the time by greasers and their like, who are just passing time. (*The Magician* by Sol Stein)[35]

Teachers in grades 4-12 can also use appropriate novels to help children and youth to learn and to practice the framing of reflective "should" questions related to societal norms. The decline in reading interests, understandings, skills, and appreciations among many of America's children and youth—due to changes in family life, the ubiquity of television, and a number of other factors—should inspire dedicated elementary and secondary social studies teachers to encourage more independent reading by learners ranging from the less able and/or reluctant readers to the gifted students desiring enrichment.

This second methodological suggestion related to the use of novels as a means of making the concept of norms more meaningful for learners could be launched easily. Using his or her own novels and borrowing pertinent books from school, public, college, and university libraries and from friends and professional colleagues, the teacher could assemble, say, 50-80 works which involve normative concerns and which would suit different student interests and reading abilities. Each class member might then be asked to choose one novel which he or she finds appealing. Next, every participant would be challenged to read a book carefully and to develop a list of 3-6 normative issues identified by or emerging from the work of fiction.

At the senior high school level, for instance, one student might select *The Siege of Silent Henry* by Lynn Hall. This novel suggests "should" questions such as these:

> Should a person surrender his or her independence for the sake of friendship and/or love?
> Should an individual put self-interest, personal profit, above honesty?
> Should one use, manipulate, others to achieve his or her goals?

In *The Siege of Silent Henry*, a high school student could use passages such as the one quoted below to generate normative issues. Robert Short, the protagonist, is caught here between conflicting norms. On the one hand, Robert's father has told him that in business it is acceptable behavior to follow a *caveat emptor* philosophy on a day-to-day basis. On the other hand, Robert's newly acquired friend, an old man by the name of Henry Lefferts, is observing that honesty is the best policy in the long run.

. . . Partly because it was so much on his mind, and partly because he was suddenly curious about Henry's reaction, Robert began to tell him about Ace [a chinchilla with defective genes], the fur-chewing babies, the problem he was faced with.

"If you were me, Henry, what would you do?"

Henry rolled his head toward Robert and opened one eye. "You asking me for advice, are you?"

Robert shrugged. "I guess so. I talked to my dad about it, and he seemed to think I'd be a sucker not to unload Ace for the three-hundred dollars."

"What's your problem then?"

Again Robert shrugged. "I don't know—it just doesn't seem to me like that would be the right thing to do. I know the really *right* thing would be to pelt Ace out, get rid of all his babies, and mark the whole thing up to experience."

"Then why don't you?"

"One thing about it," Robert called. "If I knowingly sold a fur-chewer at breeding-stock prices, it would probably give me a bad reputation later on, when I'll have other animals to sell. It might be worth it in the long run to take a loss on Ace."

"Honesty is the best policy," Henry called back.[36]

John Neufeld's *Sunday Father* is illustrative as a second novel appropriate for use in grades 10-12 which could yield "should" questions similar to the following:

Should parents stay married for the sake of their children?

With which parent should the children go? Should children be divided between their parents? Should a child have the right to choose the parent with whom he or she would like to live? How should questions such as these be decided?

Should children have anything to say about the divorce of their parents?

A number of questions regarding behavioral expectations would likely occur to the high school class member who reads these kinds of excerpts from *Sunday Father*:

"Well, if you *can* adjust to [your father's getting married again], whatever's making you so peculiar?"

"For one thing, Charlotte, it *does* mean readjusting. I mean, suddenly I'm supposed to be treated equally and I'm supposed to love everyone. I mean, it's not easy being forced to look at someone you hardly know and imagine them as a parent."

"You're not supposed to look at them equally," Charlotte said. "Surely, his new wife will come only *after* your mother. I mean, you can't just desert her."

"Like my father, you mean?"

"Ah hah!" Charlotte crowed. "That is it! You're concerned about your mother's feelings of rejection."

"Don't sound like a pint-sized Freud, please."

"But I'm right, aren't I?"

"Well," I said, thinking it out a little. "In a way. Even though we all agree that two people who can't get on any longer should live apart, still and all it's awfully soon to have found someone else. I mean it's almost an insult to my mother. He lived with her for years and years and had us and everything was supposed to have been fine and dandy all that time, and suddenly in he walks and, in effect, just announces that it's taken him almost no time at all to find someone else, someone new, or better, or just as important. It can't be very easy, taking that news, I mean."

"...I mean, just think, she gave that man the best years of her life and now she's been thrown out with the rest of the junk he'd collected in his life. It just isn't fair."

Charlotte sat silently a moment. Then, very quietly, she spoke. "Tessa, *you* don't feel that you're the junk that's been discarded, do you?

"Charlotte, you don't know what you're talking about. And neither do I....But I'll tell you one thing, if my father thinks he can just come round Sunday after Sunday and somehow behave as though he's a full-time father, he's very much mistaken. If he thinks I have to feel the same way about him now as I used to, especially after he's married, he's in for a big surprise!"[37]

A third novel, *My Name Is Asher Lev* by Chaim Potok, exemplifies a source that would be appropriate for more able senior high school students, due to its length, vocabulary demands, and conceptual level. Using this book, a class member could find a number of specific quotations which yield good normative concerns. The learner might record excerpts in one column and match "should" questions to these excerpts in a second column, as shown here:

Brief Excerpts *from the Novel*	*"Should" Questions* *Related to Norms*
... What kind of Jewish boy be-haves this way to a mother and father?...[38]	Should religion (or identification with some group along ethnic, racial, or other lines) be impor-tant in determining a person's re-lationships with his or her par-ents? With others?
... One does with a life what is precious not only to one's own self but to one's own people....[39]	Should a person live solely on the basis of his or her personal val-ues, or should he or she conduct his or her life according to the beliefs and norms of those around him or her?
... Painting is for goyim ... Jews don't draw and paint....[40]	Should art be above one's ethnic identifications, or should it be subservient to race, religion, place of national origin, current national residence, etc.?
...As an artist you are responsible to no one and to nothing, except to yourself and to the truth as you see it....[41]	Should an artist, or any other person, be responsible only to herself or himself and to her or his perception of the truth?
... Everything offends someone....[42]	Should an individual try to avoid offending others in everything that he or she does?
... Everything has a limit....[43]	Should one try to ignore and/or try to rise above any or all of the limitations others try to impose on her or him?

After each participant, in groups ranging from the fourth through the twelfth grades, has submitted a list of 3-6 normative issues based on his or her reading of an appropriate novel, the teacher might form a committee composed of those five people in the class who have the longest middle names. The five-member committee would develop and refine a master list of "should" questions, combining identical and similar concerns into single issues. The normative issues in the master list would not be arranged in any special order. The teacher could type the "should" questions on a fluid duplicator master, numbering the issues for easy reference and providing each learner with a copy for class discussion purposes. During a discussion of the duplicated list of normative issues, the teacher might ask questions such as the following:

Have you ever thought about this question? Why, or why not?

Is this question important? Why, or why not? Is it more important or less important than other questions on our list? Why?

If you wanted to work out an answer to this question, how might you go about it? Where might you get information? Might you decide by yourself what you should do? Why, or why not? If you decided to get help in answering this question, whose help might you seek? Why? What might you do if you got different kinds of advice?

What might happen to you if you could not work out an answer to this question? What might happen if you were to do the wrong thing regarding this question?

Could the right thing to do about this question be the wrong thing to do regarding another question? Why, or why not? Could the right thing to do about this question one time be the wrong thing to do at another time? Why, or why not? What should you do if different people expect you to do different things at different times regarding the same question?

Is this a question that you would like to look into and discuss as a class? Why, or why not? Is this a question that you feel we should study in committees or individually? Why, or why not?

Many novels written for children, adolescents, and adults serve beautifully as the basis for role-playing experiences. In general, role playing can clarify and vivify the sociological concept of norms. In particular, sociodrama can motivate elementary and secondary learners to reflect on beliefs and values associated with normative issues. The novel *Edgar Allan* by John Neufeld[44] is a good example of a book suited for role playing germane to "should" questions regarding norms. Innumerable behavioral expectations could emerge as class members in grades 5-12 take the parts described below.

Edgar Allan is suggested here for several reasons. The book is short and easy to read. Its characters are drawn clearly and differ with respect to their personalities and commitments. The story unfolds in such a way that the teacher could stop along the way for sociodramatic purposes, ultimately involving everyone in the class in changing situations, roles, and interpretations of roles. For the sake of illustration at this point, a teacher might read aloud in class or have her or his students individually read

Edgar Allan to the end of Chapter 15. Assuming that class members have had experience previously with role playing, the teacher could forego a long warm-up, write the simply stated issue "Should the Ficketts keep Edgar Allan?" and the names of some of the characters on the chalkboard, ask for volunteers to take given parts, and then provide each volunteer and every other class member with information such as the following, which has been written here for use at the senior high school level, but which could be adapted easily for use in lower grades:

THE REVEREND ROBERT FICKETT (FATHER): On one of your walks with Michael, your twelve-year-old son with whom you seem to have a special relationship, you have stated your belief that a whole man cannot divide his life into parts that are lived differently. You want to be a consistent person, a Christian example for others to follow. You thought that it would be good for your children, community, and church for you and your wife, Eleanor, to adopt a black child. Your wife wanted to consider everything first, to make some preparations, but you were eager to act right away in acquiring a child from an adoption agency. After you brought Edgar Allan home, your fourteen-year-old daughter, Mary Nell, was really upset. She could not believe that you would take such an important step without talking to everyone in the family. She will not play with E.A., look at him at dinner, or even speak to him. She wants to be popular with her schoolmates and friends, and she feels that you are not helping her. She says that if E.A. stays, there will be more and more trouble. She would rather leave home and move in with a girlfriend than to continue with the present situation. You have had calls from parents in your church school. Two parents transferred their children to the public schools. Two men from the church have visited you and told you that if you decide to keep Edgar Allan, the church may ask you to leave. A cross has been burned on your lawn, and M.N. knows and agrees with those who did it. The checkout ladies at the grocery store would not wait on Eleanor. [Students should be helped along the way here to see the many sanctions being applied to force conformity to norms.] You find yourself weighing Mary Nell against Edgar Allan, an impossible choice. You are pretty sure that Michael would put E.A. over M.N. You have disappointed your wife because you have not faced up to some people as she feels you should have. Michael seems confused and may have lost some respect for you already. Dinner has ended after long periods of silence. The family has gathered in the living room. What happens?

ELEANOR FICKETT (MOTHER): You like to say that God is everywhere, and you take your Christian faith seriously. You were worried from the beginning that adopting a black child would not be easy, in the years to come especially. However, you feel that there are some decisions a mother and a father have to make which they believe are right and best for their family. The parents must accept the responsibility for those decisions. You were a little surprised and disappointed in Mary Nell's reaction to Edgar Allan. You do not think that M.N. has given E.A. a fair chance. In one discussion, Mary Nell went too far, and you became angry. You want to give your family a strong commitment to honesty, the courage to do the right thing. You were both angry and sad when your husband, Robert, did not explain his position clearly and fully to the two men from the church who came to your home to see him. You were really upset about the cross burned in your front yard, but you tried to pretend everything was all right as usual. When the checkout ladies in the grocery store would not wait on you, you became angry, expressed your views, and left all of your groceries in the shopping cart. You hold that your family has the right to live the way it wants to, and that includes having Edgar Allan with you. You can stand up for yourself. But it is now time to talk all of this through. What will you say?

MARY NELL: You are fourteen years old. You are the first-born child from the marriage of Eleanor and Robert Fickett. It is bad enough being a minister's daughter, but having your parents bring a black child into your home is really ruining your life! You want very much to be popular at school. What would your friends think if you were to introduce Edgar Allan to them as your *brother?* You have tried to pretend that E.A is not around, to ignore him. You believe that people in your community have the right to live the way they want and only with the people they like. If Edgar Allan stays, Michael will get into fights, Mother will be pushed off the sidewalk or something worse, people will stop coming to Father's church, and you will leave home and never speak to your parents again. You are your parents' *real* child, not just someone they pitied and took in for silly sounding reasons. If your parents keep E.A., they will sacrifice *six* lives for *one!* That isn't fair! You are going to be heard while there is still time to return E.A.

MICHAEL: You are the twelve-year-old son of the Reverend and Mrs. Robert Fickett. You are bright and perceptive and mature for your age. Yet you do not always understand your parents. You do many things on your own, and you have a strong interest in English history. You are really O.K., but you don't have to prove it by doing things with other kids that you have been told not to. Your older sister, Mary Nell, was never all that much fun or that easy to get along with. Since the arrival of Edgar Allan, however, M.N. has been a real pain. The way she has mixed the true with the sort of false about E.A. in front of her friends has made you a bit angry. However, you agree with her that you children were old enough to be told ahead of time about Edgar Allan. Like your mother, you want to see things coming in order to prepare for them. You and your father have communicated pretty well, and you both like many of the same things; but your father has not been leveling with everyone lately. He seems to be trying to convince himself that things are the same as they always were before Edgar Allan's arrival, especially where M.N. is concerned. You have been called a "Nigger lover!" in school by Tommy Ditford and others; but you have stuck by E.A. and your principles. Father praised you for this. E.A. is happy in your home. It has been nice having another boy in your family. No one seems to care that Edgar Allan is happy and smart and cute. All that seems to matter to people is that he is black. You can't understand why Father, who wants to be a whole man, is considering returning E.A. because of pressures from the community, the church, and M.N. If the decision to adopt Edgar Allan was right in the first place, it is right now! That's one of the things you want to say.

SALLY ANN: You are almost six years old. You are tiny, bright-eyed, and funny. You are intelligent, and you see many things for a person of your age. You have a good memory, and you are very patient. Therefore, you are a natural teacher. You are delighted to have another younger brother, Edgar Allan (nearly three), whom you can teach along with Stephen Paul (almost four). You liked Edgar Allan right from the start. Something seems to be bothering Father, Mother, Mary Nell, and Michael, but you really don't understand what it is.

Checklists and scales have been used for decades to explore the presence, direction, extent, and hierarchical arrangement of opinions, attitudes, appreciations, beliefs, and values. Novels contain abundant observations, judgments, and assertions which can be used "as is" or adapted for informal instruments relevant to behavioral expectations, rules of appropriate behavior, laws, and moral codes. In this last suggestion for employing novels to study norms, the teacher might try his or her hand at using a book such as *Flowers for Algernon* by Daniel Keyes[45] to get ideas for items that could be created in first-draft form for a scale ranging from "STRONGLY DISAGREE" (SD), to "DISAGREE" (D), on through "UNCERTAIN" (U), to "AGREE" (A), and "STRONGLY AGREE" (SA).

	SD	D	U	A	SA
1. The more intelligent a person is, the more problems and unhappy experiences he or she has in a society.	___	___	___	___	___
2. It is better to have friends who make fun of you than it is to be without friends.	___	___	___	___	___
3. It would be worth it for a person to sacrifice his or her life in order to make a really important contribution to science.	___	___	___	___	___
4. It would be better to be really intelligent and to have a shorter life than it would be to have a low level of intelligence and to live a longer life.	___	___	___	___	___
5. A person should avoid any information or educational experience which might cause him or her to question his or her religion.	___	___	___	___	___
6. All education should be practical, useful. A person should not learn anything just for the sake of learning, just because she or he is curious.	___	___	___	___	___
7. It would be better to have average intelligence and to be popular than it would be to have superior intelligence and to be unpopular.	___	___	___	___	___
8. It is better to have loved and lost than never to have loved at all.	___	___	___	___	___

9. A person has to be intelligent in order to be considered as a real human being.   ___ ___ ___ ___ ___

10. A person has a better life if she or he works at something unimportant and safe than if she or he tries to do something that is important and uncertain.   ___ ___ ___ ___ ___

11. It is what one does for others in life that matters; not what one does for one's self.   ___ ___ ___ ___ ___

12. It is better to live a rich, short life than it is to live an empty, long life.   ___ ___ ___ ___ ___

13. There should be limits on the kinds of research which scientists can conduct. Some questions or problems should not be investigated.   ___ ___ ___ ___ ___

14. Applied research is more important than pure research.   ___ ___ ___ ___ ___

15. A person should pursue the truth wherever it leads her or him.   ___ ___ ___ ___ ___

16. Intelligence, education, and knowledge are not worth anything unless they are balanced by love.   ___ ___ ___ ___ ___

After the teacher has prepared the initial version of the scale, she or he should give every class member a reproduced copy to read and to edit carefully. Items could be rewritten, discarded, combined, and added by the group until a better scale has been developed. Then, every learner might be asked to complete a copy of the form without identifying himself or herself. The responses would next be tabulated and the distribution for each item discussed thoroughly. The teacher might ask questions similar to these:

Why do you suppose there was such strong agreement on this item?

There were more uncertain reactions on various items than any other of the columns. Why do you think this was the case?

This is the only item where there was unanimous disagreement. How many possibilities can you suggest which might help to explain this position?

There was rather strong agreement with respect to the fifth item on our scale but strong disagreement in many instances with the eleventh item. Could there be an inconsistency here? Why, or why not?

Etc.

If the class discussion should be open and lively enough, the same scale could be administered a second time to see if any responses might be changed. Any substantial alterations would be discussed thoroughly. Follow-up activities could include having students select one item about which they would like to write a position statement, to form small discussion groups around five or six of the most interesting, controversial, and/or significant items, to work up a role-playing situation around the best item, to form five or six committees which could develop scales for five or six other novels, and so on. Although the illustration offered here was developed with senior high school students in mind, it should be obvious to the creative classroom teacher that adaptation for different grade levels would not be difficult.

Conclusion

By helping learners to investigate the socialization process and to consider the concept of norms, the elementary or secondary social studies teacher may make a contribution, however small, toward advancing the "good health" of the society envisaged by Edward C. Banfield in *The Unheavenly City Revisited*. Banfield writes that it is difficult

> to indicate in a sentence or two what is meant by the "good health" of the society. The ability of the society to maintain itself as a going concern is certainly a primary consideration; so is its free and democratic character. In the last analysis, however, the quality of a society must be judged by its tendency to produce desirable human types; the healthy society, then, is one that not only stays alive but also moves in the direction of giving greater scope and expression to what is distinctively human.... [46]

Notes

1. Jack D. Douglas, "The Relevance of Sociology," in *The Relevance of Sociology*, ed. Jack D. Douglas (New York: Appleton-Century-Crofts, 1970), p. 185.
2. Judson R. Landis, *Sociology: Concepts and Characteristics*, 3rd ed. (Belmont, Calif.: Wadsworth Publishing Co., 1977), p. 74.
3. Lucile Duberman, *Gender and Sex in Society* (New York: Praeger Publishers, 1975), p. 25.
4. Barbara Robinson, *The Best Christmas Pageant Ever* (New York: Harper & Row, 1972), pp. 1, 7, 14.
5. Adrienne Richard, *Pistol* (New York: Dell Publishing Co., 1970), pp. 31, 32, 37.
6. Duberman, *Gender and Sex in Society*, p. 26.
7. Louise Fitzhugh, *Nobody's Family Is Going to Change* (New York: Dell Publishers, 1974), p. 52.
8. Scott O'Dell, *Carlota* (Boston: Houghton Mifflin, 1977), p. 15.
9. Howard S. Rowland, *No More School* (New York: E. P. Dutton & Co., 1975), pp. ix, xi.
10. Clarence Darrow, *The Story of My Life* (New York: Charles Scribner's Sons, 1932), pp. 18, 19, 25.
11. Golda Meir, *My Life* (New York: Dell Publishing Co., 1976), pp. 26, 27, 28, 30, 32.
12. Dick Gregory with Robert Lipsyte, *Nigger: An Autobiography* (New York: E. P. Dutton & Co. 1965), pp. 45-46.
13. Mary Kay Phelan, *Probing the Unknown: The Story of Dr. Florence Sabin* (New York: Dell Publishing Co., 1976), p. 33.
14. Leslie Alexander Lacy, *Cheer the Lonesome Traveler: The Life of W. E. B. Du Bois* (New York: Dell Publishing Co., 1972), pp. 20-21.
15. Raymond H. Muessig, *Discussion Pictures for Beginning Social Studies* (New York: Harper & Row, 1967).

16. "America's New Manners," *Time* 112, no. 22 (November 27, 1978): 64, 65, 75.

17. Amy Vanderbilt and Letitia Baldridge, *The Amy Vanderbilt Complete Book of Etiquette: A Guide to Contemporary Living: Revised and Expanded by Letitia Baldridge* (Garden City, N.Y.: Doubleday & Co., 1978), pp. xi, xii-xiii, 38.

18. Betty Baker, *Killer-of-Death* (New York: Dell Publishing Co., 1974), pp. 50, 60, 61.

19. Clarice Stasz Stoll, *Female & Male: Socialization, Social Roles, and Social Structure,* 2d ed. (Dubuque, Iowa: Wm. C. Brown Co., 1978), p. 72.

20. Gail Sheehy, *Passages: Predictable Crises of Adult Life* (New York: Bantam Books, 1977), pp. 14, 37, 54.

21. John B. Williamson, Jerry F. Boren, and Linda Evans, "Introduction: The Sociology of Social Problems," in *Social Problems: The Contemporary Debates,* 2d ed., ed. John B. Williamson, Jerry F. Boren, and Linda Evans (Boston: Little, Brown and Co., 1977), p. 17.

22. Chaim Potok, *My Name Is Asher Lev* (Greenwich, Conn.: Fawcett Publications, 1973), p. 248.

23. Vera and Bill Cleaver, *Grover* (New York: The New American Library, 1975), p. 65.

24. Lynn Hall, *The Siege of Silent Henry* (New York: Avon Books, 1977), p. 92.

25. Florence Parry Heide, *When the Sad One Comes to Stay* (Philadelphia: J. B. Lippincott Co., 1975), p. 14.

26. Claude Berri, *The Two of Us* (New York: Popular Library, 1968), p. 44.

27. Bette Greene, *Summer of My German Soldier* (New York: Bantam Books, 1974), p. 139.

28. Fitzhugh, *Nobody's Family Is Going to Change,* p. 10.

29. John Neufeld, *Sunday Father* (New York: The New American Library, 1976), p. 33.

30. Isabelle Holland, *The Man Without a Face* (Philadelphia: J. B. Lippincott Co., 1972), p. 150.

31. John R. Tunis, *His Enemy, His Friend* (New York: Avon Books, 1970), p. 144.

32. Muriel Spark, *The Prime of Miss Jean Brodie* (New York: Dell Publishing Co., 1966), p. 18.

33. Daniel Keyes, *Flowers for Algernon* (New York: Bantam Books, 1967), pp. 138-39.

34. Winifred Madison, *Growing Up in a Hurry* (Boston: Little, Brown and Co., 1973), p. 161.

35. Sol Stein, *The Magician* (New York: Dell Publishing Co., 1972), p. 191.

36. Hall, *The Siege of Silent Henry,* pp. 99-100.

37. Neufeld, *Sunday Father,* (New York: The New American Library, 1976), pp. 82-85.

38. Potok, *My Name Is Asher Lev,* p. 112.

39. Ibid, p. 128.

40. Ibid., p. 164.

41. Ibid., p. 208.

42. Ibid., p. 289.

43. Ibid., p. 342.

44. John Neufeld, *Edgar Allan* (New York: The New American Library, 1969).

45. Keyes, *Flowers for Algernon.*

46. Edward C. Banfield, *The Unheavenly City Revisited* (Boston: Little, Brown and Co., 1974), p. 9.

Index